Calm Kids

LIFESTYLE

Calm Kids

Shirley Lane-Smith

GEDDES & GROSSET

Published 2007 by Geddes & Grosset, David Dale House,
New Lanark, ML11 9DJ, Scotland
First Published 2004, reprinted 2007

First published in Australia in 2000 by Thomas C. Lothian Pty Ltd

ISBN 978 1 84205 347 8

Printed and bound in Poland

POLSKABOOK

CONTENTS

ACKNOWLEDGEMENTS

This book is the result of two years' work and a life-time of experience. It might never have been finished except for a recent illness—an illness that was to draw so many people into my life. These people have been inspirational in making me finish that which is very dear to my heart—my passion.

All at once life threw real challenges my way; the loss of a love, heartache with my children, strains on friendships, health problems, overload of work, money worries, relationship problems from my past, and my body, mind and soul slowed down.

I dedicate this book to my dad who came to my rescue, as dads do. This book would not have been possible without his encouragement and his total faith in me. I also dedicate this book to my mum who let dad come to my rescue. I value all my mother has done in her life. She is truly a woman who has made her mark in the world by doing what she believed in.

I also dedicate this book to my brothers. Without them I would not have learnt unconditional love. To both of you I thank you for being in my life.

And to all my friends and lovers, past and present: times and situations change, we change, but time has taught me there are some special people who really do care. To each and every one of you lots of love, hugs and kisses. Thank you for being there whenever I needed your support.

Finally, I dedicate this book to my children. Without them this book would have little substance. From the moment they were conceived, I have learnt much about life and about being a parent. We have been through a great deal together and their love and support is my driving force.

The love, care and support I receive from my parents and my children is overwhelming. I am deeply honoured to share my life with you, and send you my deepest, heartfelt thanks.

OUR UNIVERSAL PLEDGE

> Whether made in love, greed, hate or need each life has a purpose to fulfil.
>
> In many Eastern cultures it is said that a pledge is made in the heavenly skies for each soul's needs on Earth and that all those who cross a soul's path are connected; each needed to help, guide and teach the soul along life's path to the completion of all earthly duties.

When your baby was born did you ever stop to wonder what happened to the manual on how to bring up your child and be a good parent? The one with all the how tos, why fors and whenevers explained. I've had three children and my manual never arrived!

The fact that you are reading this book shows you are on a quest to be the best parent you can. You may be asking yourself how you will cope with the overwhelming pressures and responsibilities of family life. You may already have experienced the pressures of your children's school life, or the breakdown of a partnership or marriage, and be asking yourself, 'How can I be successful in the workplace and remain sane?' As we don our different hats for our different roles, many of us push ourselves to the limit. Sometimes when the pressure becomes too much, frustration and despair set in. Especially when our children are not coping, or if our relationship with them is not as good as we hoped for. You'll be pleased to know that you are not alone.

Successful parenting

How can we juggle all these things and be effective and positive parents? What can we do to help our children be more successful and lead better stress-free lives? First, we must accept there are many ways to be a successful parent. Each family is different: a different mother and father each with their own genetic inheritance, beliefs, values, background, culture and education. What might work for one family doesn't necessarily work for another. You have to make that judgement, but there are a few starting places, and my best advice is to find practical ways to help you and your children manage day-to-day challenges in a way that suits you.

Remember that as guardians it is your responsibility to guide your children to their highest path or purpose. They are on loan to you for a short time and they are not yours to keep. As a parent we cannot walk our children's paths for them or impose our unfulfilled dreams upon them. We are each responsible for our own life. Our children are special and unique, needing to be nurtured and attended to as individuals. We need to instil guidelines and values in our children from birth. We need to learn and live by our family's moral code, be given religious and spiritual guidance, and be allowed the freedom of choice and right to expression.

By helping your children deal with life's challenges and opportunities instead of suppressing their thoughts and emotions, you will help your children become confident, successful adults. You will also be helping yourself and your family, as each person in your family supports the others. It is interesting how we look and strive for success in many areas of our lives when so often we do not look and strive for success as a family. How often do we pat ourselves on the back for a job well done, when each one of us relies on the family team to work towards a common goal?

Being a parent is not an easy task and can be quite daunting at times. It means taking responsibility for the health and wellbeing of another person. It is our responsibility to realise, acknowledge and use our own personal power and apply it within the family. The more self-developed we are ourselves the more self-developed our children will be. They are mirrors of ourselves.

There is a lot of information on positive parenting and how to bring up your children, but have you ever thought to trust in your own judgement? If you are like the majority of parents you handled your firstborn with kid gloves. Every time she sneezed she was rushed off to the doctor, the herbalist, the naturopath . . . Come child number two or three, you find you are more relaxed. But have you ever asked yourself why you rely so much on the opinions of others instead of looking within for the answers? Have you thought to rely on your intuition or gut feeling? Have you asked your children what they feel they need?

Responsible parenting

Responsible parenting means looking at both your life and your children's lives and working at being a successful family team. It is about looking at the basic principles of life and applying them. When the principles are out of kilter they need to be looked at and repaired by all members of the family. If one person in the family is having a problem, then other members will also be experiencing problems. We cannot heal one alone, we must heal the whole family. What this means is that you as a parent have to be very honest with yourself. You have to be open and prepared for change. As do the rest of your family.

So what are the basic principles of life?

Love Not just the feeling or the impulse but the principle. You can be the meanest person in the world but you can still act with the intention of love. This must come from the heart not the head. Sometimes we do things that are actions of love but are not really from the heart.

Freedom Being true to yourself. If you are living your life without facades then you are free to be the real you. Too many times we hide behind what we think people want us to be instead of just being ourselves.

Order We all need to have parameters or guidelines by which to live. When we have guidelines we know what we can live with and find acceptable for peace of mind.

Honour Honouring ourselves and others, respecting each other's boundaries. We are not all the same. What is right for you is different for someone else.

Trust Use your intuition or gut feeling in every area of your life and trust and pray that what you are given in your life is right for you. I believe that we are never given more than we can cope with, no matter how bad.

If one or more of these principles is not being lived by, by any member of the family, then the family becomes dysfunctional. When this happens we experience lack of self-esteem, self-love, self-motivation, sense of self and loss of creative self-expression, which leads to negative behaviour.

The idea of this book is to introduce and share practical tools, ideas and therapies with you and your children to build a happy successful family. These treatments are down-to-earth treatments that deal with and care for the soul. As you and your children work together you will both benefit and grow, developing a positive outlook, focusing your thoughts, feelings and creativity into a higher level of performance and self-satisfaction. These treatments will give your family direction, meaning, purpose, fulfilment, wholeness and a lot of happiness.

Let me now share with you how I began my quest to become an effective parent; a single mother, running my own business. Then I'll share some ideas and techniques that have worked for me, and my family, as well as many others I have come across in my travels.

My story, not his-story

Each one of us has a mission and a purpose to fulfil in this lifetime. From where I stand in my life I have finally learnt there are no accidents. Everything happens for a reason. Everything we have done, everyone we have met and everything we have thought and felt has made us what we are today. No experience has been lost.

I was born in postwar England, the eldest of three children. My youngest brother was intellectually disabled, but due to my parents' true dedication, and to their credit, he never had to live in an institution. Sadly, a few years ago my youngest brother died, but his memory lives on in my heart. He was very special and unique and enriched each member of my family in their own way. For me, the experience tested and stretched us, but it also joined and united us. The gift he gave me was how to give and receive love. My other brother's gift to me, apart from his undying love and support, was to introduce me to Buddhism over 20 years ago, which was the beginning of my spiritual quest.

Childhood taught me a great deal including how to deal with the practical side of life as well as having an appreciation for the finer things. One event that clouded my path was the death of my grandmother when I was 12 years of age. She had been like a mother to me.

As a teenager I met a handsome, suave university student who introduced me to the world of drugs. Despite my solid upbringing and defying all my core values, I tried a concoction of drugs. For two and a half years I was an addict.

I am a perfectionist and I took the world pretty seriously even at a young age. I had great hopes, dreams and expectations of myself. My final years at school were strenuous and I found myself overloaded with work. I popped more and more pills to keep me going with my studies and more still to keep me going over very busy social weekends. It all became too much but I felt I could sort it all out on my own. I thought the only way to get my life back on track was to quit school; leave my boyfriend, because he was my link to the drug scene; leave home, and go cold turkey, which I don't recommend to anyone. I also tried to commit suicide because I felt I was losing sight of all my goals and dreams. In the end, I got engaged and I went to live in Holland for two years, but when the romance began to fall apart I became anorexic, my weight going from 52 kg to just under 40 kg. I was picked up off the floor many times because I had fainted from low blood pressure and anaemia.

After returning to England I went from 40 kg to around 70 kg, which gave me another hurdle to jump, testing me to my limits. I hated who I had become and what I was doing to myself. I had no direction and I was breaking up inside. Then I found love, went to Australia, and had a new direction in life, one with purpose and meaning. I was married for 17 years, a life that was to take me on many different routes, some devastating, but others extremely rewarding. My three children being the biggest gift of all. In 1992, we travelled around Australia for seven and a half months in which time we really got to know each other and ourselves. My three children are now teenagers and are loving, caring and supportive people.

A parent's role

My experience helps other parents and their children because it is the real stuff. I have been there and I have done it and survived. I know that whatever happens we are never given more than we can truly face and deal with. It may be hard and seem overwhelming but when we get to the other side and look back it has all happened for our personal growth.

As a parent you are where you are today because of what

you have done in your life. Bringing your children into this world is not always going to be easy but it is up to us to love, care and support these little ones, guiding them along their path in the direction that is best for them. If they stumble and fall pick them up and dust them off. They are part of you but they are not you. They are individuals that need to see the positives to life whatever befalls them. Life is forever changing and we all need to adapt our lives to fit our desires and needs.

Your children are only with you for a very short time so treasure it and try to enjoy them as much as you can. Our children are often the best teachers and can bring out the child within ourselves. Have fun with them. Whatever sort of parent you are, or think you are, the fact that you have picked up this book shows you care for the wellbeing of your children and yourself. In the following chapters I would like to share with you some insights that I hope will help you and your children build a better tomorrow.

Thoughts of comfort and wisdom for your journey as a parent

- Everything we do, everyone we meet, everything we think and feel has made us who we are today and will continue to take us along the path of life. Everything happens for a reason.
- Each one of us has a purpose, a mission to fulfil, we need to find it and take it with both hands.
- It is our choice which road we take, who we walk it with, why, and how.
- If we don't like the path we are on we must take responsibility and change it.
- Life's lessons are presented to help us change direction in our lives and to help us grow. If we can face them and deal with them positively we can move on to other lessons, otherwise like the bad penny, they'll keep turning up.

- Sometimes we have to make sacrifices for others but usually it is in our best interests too.
- Look out for synchronicities, the signposts of your life's path are there.
- Although we are our children's teachers, our pupils teach us.
- What we learn we can teach our children. They are aware little people.
- Give them the responsibility of life instead of carrying their life on your shoulders.
- Children are only on loan to us, not ours to keep.
- Being a parent, or an adult around children, is a wonderful opportunity to experience our inner child. Their lives are precious, unique and special. We are here to guide them along life's path.
- Trust your heart, and follow it.

What makes a successful family?

Successful families need participants who are:

- communicative
- self-developed both as individuals and also as team workers
- supportive and encouraging
- honest and open
- reliable and trustworthy
- flexible and tolerant
- sharing, caring, and loving
- ready to share the good and bad times giving space when needed
- encouraging of interdependence rather than dependence
- able to see the good in others and to celebrate each member's achievements
- true to themselves and others.

Part One

Developing the Gift of Inner Peace

INTRODUCTION

Alternative solutions

This book provides personal insights and some answers to the many and varied challenges that you and your children may encounter along your path together. Along with generous doses of practical advice I introduce and explain the use of seven alternative therapies that I have found highly successful for myself, my family and other children and adults. Of course there are many different ways you can work with your children to help them build healthy, balanced and successful mental, physical and spiritual lives, and it is your choice which you use.

In Part Two, you will find descriptions and information about these seven therapies; all of which I recommend to you as tools to enhance your life. By researching and learning more about each one of these, and the many others that may be of interest to you, you will grow as a parent and as a person. The therapies I have chosen are:

1. Affirmations and prayer
2. Aromatherapy
3. Australian Bush Flower Essences
4. Journalling
5. Kinergetics

6. Massage
7. Meditation

As you go through the different emotions and situations I have described here, you will discover some new ways and ideas to implement these seven therapies for you and your children. I am particularly concerned to heal both parents and children. If you are not whole and complete how can you expect your children to be?

As individuals we are all striving to be seen and heard. I believe in this, the 21st century, too many children are having their spiritual side and their individuality quashed in order to conform with 'society'. However, we are beginning to recognise the need for our children to express their individuality. As parents our divine role is to help them accomplish their needs and desires, giving them a sense of self-gratification and recognition. Every child has a voice that needs to be acknowledged.

1
TOXIC PARENTING

Children are wondrous gifts lent to us for a short time. When small they are full of magic, innocence, love and honesty. As they grow, they form their own opinions and want instant gratification. At times they try us beyond belief, but all we have to do is look into their eyes to see that nothing can replace the love between a parent and a child.

Parental behaviour

Our children watch what we do and follow the example we set. As children, we take our experiences into our adult life and we often want to change things about ourselves we don't like. Sometimes situations challenge us. At these times we behave 'out of character'. Perhaps turning to alcohol, smoking, or drugs, but these affect our home life. When we are troubled our children sense that something isn't right. We must never try to hide our feelings. I have learnt to accept my feelings and experiences, and allow that what is happening no matter how difficult is simply meant to be. If people around you cannot understand what you are going through that is okay. Your children are with you for life. But at times when we face a personal crisis we can fall into the trap of toxic parenting.

Toxic parenting describes people who abuse their children

whether intentionally or unintentionally, consciously or subconsciously. This abuse comes in many forms; physical, mental, sexual, through use of control tactics, or through parental drug or alcohol abuse. Some parents try and live out their dreams through their children because they have unfulfilled dreams from their own childhood. As parents our role is to learn how to take responsibility for ourselves and our children, but after a short time we must learn to let our children be free to be themselves, while we continue with our lives. How your children react when you are not dealing with life in a positive way depends on you.

I recently had an experience where my daughter's friend called me weird. 'You're a weird mum,' she said. I was weird in her eyes because I was not like her parents who she felt restricted her thoughts and her feelings. As a child I felt I couldn't talk to my mum about a lot of things and the child who called me 'weird' feels the same. There are still a lot of old-fashioned ways that many of us hold on to because of our upbringing, religion, education and so on. When I look at how the young people of today act and react it's so different from my experience. Today children seem more open to friendship and communication. As a child I always wanted to be on the phone and be in touch with friends, but children today really do get in touch with their friends.

Today children allow others into their lives and their feelings. People ask me how I got into this profession. Well, I became fed up with helping 40-year-old friends who were trying to heal their relationships and rebuild their lives. We try to protect our children from what they are going through, when the best we can do is share their experiences, and listen to what is happening in their lives.

What you can do to feel good about yourself while your children are experiencing the ups and downs of life

A checklist of things to help you to be a calm parent

1. Do things that make you feel happy and relaxed, such as luxuriating in a warm bath by candlelight with soft music playing.
2. Take the time out of your busy schedule to burn essential oils and meditate.
3. Take a walk on the beach or the park and get in touch with nature; another form of meditation.
4. Have a massage, spa or sauna regularly to help you unwind.
5. Exercise in any shape or form that you enjoy. Make it a part of your lifestyle rather than just something you think you need to do.
6. Go for beauty treatments and aromatherapy sessions when you feel you need them.
7. Read an inspiring book or work on your journal.
8. Practise positive affirmations and break any habit you may have of putting yourself down.
9. Allow yourself to grow with your children; you are on your own path of self-development too!
10. Set yourself goals. Plan a time for them to be realised and make them happen.
11. Be prepared to ask for help if and when you need it. Never be too proud.
12. Fill your days with things you have a passion for. We all need to feel passion for the things we enjoy.
13. Help other people when you can. By helping others we give service to the community and it always comes back somehow. You never know when you may need another friendly face around you.

14. Expand your mind in ways that broaden your knowledge. Our ideas need to be expanded and education in any form is a benefit.
15. Do things that make you laugh and have a really good laugh.

If you do most of the things on this list, your life will be more satisfying. Most important of all, be yourself and accept you have feelings, emotions and faults. Don't be scared of who you really are. Get to know yourself and understand that if the people around you don't like you for something you do or say then it's time to move on and form new friendships. Your children have chosen you just as you have chosen them. But remember if you are experiencing trauma, your children have the right to react in their own way.

Some guidelines that will help your children when you are facing a personal crisis

It is important to give your children some guidance on how they can react if you have handled your personal problems badly and fallen off the rails. Control is not the answer. Your children need to be able to express themselves as individuals with good self-esteem to deal with conflict. They need to be able to express themselves in order to face what is happening in their own lives. If you are confronted by your children it is important you follow some guidelines to make sure neither of you are scarred by the experience.

1. Don't get cross or angry with them for expressing their feelings and venting their emotions. Their feelings need to be brought out into the open.
2. Don't lash out at the expression of their emotions. It will only make them keep their feelings locked inside and they will fear opening up to you.

3. Don't punish them because of what they may have said or done in the heat of the moment. It doesn't make the problem go away.
4. If your children bring up what they feel in public, don't belittle them or put them down. It only makes both of you look and feel small.
5. Don't try to get even. You may feel that you have been put in your place by a 'little' person but to try and get even for actions done is counterproductive.

If your children tell you something they feel is important for their livelihood—listen. Take note of their concerns and see if you can find the truth in it before you judge. Perhaps that 'little' person is giving you a heavenly message that may change your life.

I have found all the alternative therapies outlined in this book most effective in daily use as a parent. It is important to make time for yourself; spoil yourself and keep your life focused and your children will follow your example.

Boost your confidence

Some positive sayings to boost your self-esteem and confidence

- I am a wonderful person and am bringing my children up t o the best of my ability.
- I make the right decisions for myself with clarity and success.
- I am who I am and I draw situations and people to me for my highest purpose.
- I am love.

The looking mirror

A meditation to boost your morale and your self-esteem

Take three long deep breaths. Let your shoulders drop and your neck relax. Clear your mind of any thoughts and just try to be.

Imagine yourself standing in your favourite place. It doesn't matter where you are, but you must feel it and see it. As you stand there, imagine a huge rainbow, full of every colour you can think of. Depending on what you need at this moment some colours may be stronger than others but just allow them to be. See these colours coming down towards you, reaching out to touch you. Feel them or see them encompass you totally and completely. Allow the swirls of colour to engulf you. As this happens the sun comes out to play and warms your heart, mind, body and soul; feel its warmth. The sun makes the colours even stronger and you can now feel the energy of life running through you.

Now imagine you are standing in front of a long mirror. Take a really good look at the person standing there.

This is you.

Take time to acknowledge that now. Tell this person you love them and you thank them for everything they have done to get you where you are. Rainbows of colour flow from the mirror straight through you filling you even more. Feel nature's healing qualities as you become one with nature.

The person you see in the mirror is who you have become because of many lifetimes of experience. Ask for the knowledge you need to be able to see each day as special. Ask for the people and the situations you need to help you develop and to complete your mission in life. If you feel you don't have a purpose or direction in life at this time ask what you are meant to do and why. Feel the warm rays engulf you totally and utterly. Watch what unfolds within you and listen for the reply to your questions. If you have problems with your children ask what you can do to help make the situation better. Listen for the reply.

If there are things you wish to achieve and are not sure how to go about it ask now. Listen and absorb what is being said to you. Ask for guidance as the colours pour through you making you feel warm, loved, whole and at peace. Feel your courage, strength and conviction pouring over and through you giving you knowledge of what must be done. See your pathway with clarity.

Suggested Australian Bush Flower Essences

To relieve anxiety: Dog Rose and Crowea
To overcome addictions: Bottlebrush, Waratah, Red Lily, Sundew, Flannel Flower and Five Corners
To restore balance: Jacaranda, Bush Fuchsia and Crowea
To fight depression: Kapok Bush, Waratah, Tall Yellow Top, and Red Grevillea
To overcome fatigue: Macrocarpa, Sunshine Wattle, and Old Man Banksia
To release frustration: Old Man Banksia, Black-eyed Susan, Jacaranda, Sunshine Wattle, Red Grevillea, Wild Potato Bush
For disorders of the liver: Mountain Devil, Dagger Hakea, Southern Cross and Slender Rice Flower
To reduce nervousness and restore calm: Dog Rose, Black-eyed Susan and Jacaranda
To reduce cigarette smoking: Boronia and Bottlebrush
To treat toxicity: Mountain Devil, Slender Rice Flower, Dagger Hakea, Spinifex, Bush Iris, Lymph, Bottlebrush, Dog Rose

Getting to know you and your family

In Part Two, the chapter 'Journal Your Life's Journey' describes the importance and effectiveness of journalling. You may like to try the following journalling exercises by yourself or with your family in order to help each member understand themselves a little better. It is important the answers are honest—you must be true to yourself. Keep these exercises and look at them at a later date to see if they need to be changed or how they have changed. When you read them ask yourself if there is any room for more personal improvement.

For parents

Do you know who you really are? (An exercise in journalling)

1. Do you know who you are? Describe yourself. Describe how others see you.
2. Do you like the person you are? Describe your best qualities. Describe some of your faults. What makes you special?
3. Do you know your family? Describe some of the qualities you see in other family members. How do these qualities enrich your life?
4. How many of your beliefs and values are being realised within your family?
5. What would you like to change in your family? How can you make these changes? How will they affect other members of your family?

Getting to know me

1. Give a brief description of yourself, physically and spiritually. The real you including all your good points and your bad points.
2. Describe each one of your family members. Remember to include both their good and bad points.
3. Describe how all the members of your family live, work and play together as a family.
4. Describe your relationship with your partner. How can it be enhanced?

5. Outline your desires, goals and dreams.
6. How does each member of your family fit into your dreams and goals?
7. What motivates you? What can you do to enhance your motivation?
8. Do you take time out for yourself? What do you do? How can you enhance this valuable time?
9. What do you do as a family to relax? How can you make better use of this precious time?
10. Are you happy in your relationships? How could you improve your relationships?
11. Are you enjoying your work? Does it satisfy you? How can you improve it?
12. What are your fears? How can you overcome them?

Getting to know your children

1. What do you think your children want for you?
2. Write down what you feel you can do for your children.
3. Write down how you can get to know your children better.
4. What sort of adults do you want your children to become?
5. Write down the qualities and characteristics you would like to see them develop and how.
6. What dreams do you have for your children? Are they your dreams or theirs?
7. What do you think your children desire for themselves?
8. Do your children take time to relax? If so, how? How can they enhance their relaxation time?
9. How much time do you spend with each person individually and as a family over the course of a week or per day? How can you improve or enhance that time?
10. Do you communicate openly and honestly? How can you improve your communication?

11. Write down six things that make you a wonderful mother or father.

For your children

Getting to know myself (An exercise in journalling)

1. Describe or draw how you see yourself.
2. Describe or draw your mum.
3. Describe or draw your dad.
4. Describe your brothers or sisters. What do you like about your siblings? What do you dislike about them? How do they make you feel?
5. Write down all the things you are good at. Write down all the things you think you are not good at.
6. Write down some of the feelings you like. Why? Write down some of the feelings you don't like. Why not?
7. What are you frightened of?
8. Do you speak honestly and openly with your mum or dad? How can you begin to speak openly and honestly with your mum or dad if you're not doing that now?
9. Do you feel that mum or dad is honest with you?
10. What dreams would you like to come true?
11. Do you feel good about yourself? If not, why?
12. Do you take the time to play quietly by yourself or just sit and be quiet? If you want to be quiet where do you go? Where would you like to go?
13. What does your family do together? What would you like to do together?
14. Do you have lots of friends? Are they good friends?
15. Do you like school? What is your best subject? Why?
16. If you could grant a wish for mummy what would it be?
17. If you could grant a wish for daddy what would it be?
18. What do you want to do when you have grown up? What sort of person would you like to be? (For example,

which words would describe the person you want to be: happy, sad, angry, helpful, strong, clever, quick, funny, quiet, loud, serious, slow, warm, cool, hard, soft, big, little, nice, nasty, polite, rude, calm, spirited, etc.)

19. Write down six things that make you a wonderful daughter or son.

For teenagers

Getting to know myself (An exercise in journalling)

1. Give a brief description of yourself, physically and emotionally—the real you—including all your good points and your bad points.
2. Describe each one of your family members, including their good and bad points.
3. Describe how you feel you fit into the family.
4. Describe your relationship with your sisters or brothers. How can it be improved?
5. How do they make you feel? Why?
6. Outline your desires, goals and dreams.
7. What motivates you? What can you do to enhance your motivation?
8. Do you take time out for yourself? What do you do? How can you use this valuable time better?
9. Do you take enough time to enhance your own personal growth? For instance, do you read books, go to seminars, talks, support clubs and so on?
10. What do you do as a family to relax?
11. How much time can you make to share with your family?
12. Do you take time to relax? If so, how? How can you enhance this time?
13. What do you want for your parents?
14. What sort of adult do you want to be? Write down the

qualities and characteristics you would like to develop and how.

15. What do you feel are your boundaries and limitations?
16. Are you frightened of anything?
17. Are you true to yourself? Are you true to your family? How can you enhance that?
18. Can you speak honestly with your parents? (If not, write down how you might be able to change this.)
19. Do you like school? What is your best subject?
20. How do you feel about the opposite sex?
21. How can you develop your relationships with others?
22. How do you think your parents feel about you?
23. When your emotions get a little out of hand how would you like your parents to respond?
24. How should your parents share advice with you? (For instance, would you like to hear how they dealt with problems as a teenager or how they felt?)
25. Do you feel that your parents understand you? How can you help them to understand you better?
26. Write down six things that make you a wonderful teenager.

Trust in what is being given to you and do something positive to make yourself, your life and your relationships happier, more fulfilling, successful and more fun. In this chapter we have looked at what makes you tick. Now let's look at what you can do to help your children grow into healthy adults. First, we have to provide them with a suitable education and help them become aware of what life has to offer. Then they will be ready to make important choices about their personalities and their lives.

2
EDUCATION

Children have inquisitive minds that must be planted with positive seeds of thought to blossom and grow, bearing all the fruits of life.

A smarter way of thinking

In the previous chapter we learnt something important about ourselves as parents: how we are and what we do has an influence on our children. Our role as parents is to educate our children in a way that is beneficial for them so they may grow into successful, healthy adults. Choosing the right school for your children is an important part of your role in their education. Most parents don't have the time or the resources to execute this role thoroughly. The education your children receive will form a major part of their upbringing, and in today's society it is increasingly difficult for parents to spend time with their children, especially with homework. Our lives are busy. In many two-parent families both parents have jobs outside the home. Many children have extra-curricular school subjects to pursue and their homework load seems greater than ever.

The school your children attend is not always the one of your choice. You may want to send your children to private schools but can't afford to. Both state and private schools educate our future adults to the best of their ability. Some parents prefer private schools because they may offer other benefits like extra facilities, better discipline and more parental input. In addition, if children aren't performing, or are struggling, a private school is more likely to take immediate action to rectify the situation because the parents are paying school fees and expect their children's needs to be met. Many private schools have a better record of academic results. On the other hand, state schools better prepare children for everyday life and the financial outlay is often not as great compared with most private schools' fees.

The decision of whether your children should attend a co-educational school or a single-sex school also has to be made. Personally I am very glad I went to an all-girls' school because having boys around may have put me off some of my school work. Some considerations to be weighed are: whether your child is an only child, or whether he/she has brothers and sisters to interact with.

A recent survey showed the more parents are involved with their children's school, the better their children's academic marks are. Children love to see mum or dad helping out in the school. Some parents may prefer to become part of the school's parent-teacher association or school board. I have spent a lot of time on committees and found them most rewarding, but committees are not for everyone. You may decide to try and spend time with your children while they are doing their homework, or when they have a special assignment to complete. It is important to show an interest in what your children are doing at school, or in their studies, even if you don't understand their school work.

Homework

I have a few guidelines that I follow to make homework less stressful for my children:

1. Show an interest in what they are doing. For instance, ask them what they find hard or easy about the subject they are studying.
2. Try to get your children into a study routine. Impose strict rules and guidelines about what time of day homework is done; for instance, they should have all their homework done before they are allowed to turn on the television.
3. Help them to plan for exams well ahead of time. Put up a wall chart of the calendar year in the area where they study and mark in their examination dates.
4. Don't push them, especially if they are final year students.
5. Encourage your children to do five minutes of meditation before they start studying. Meditation will help them concentrate and absorb information more readily.
6. Give them a snack when they first come home from school to keep up their energy levels. Food will help them concentrate better. Let them know when their main meal is going to be ready, so they can plan their time accordingly.
7. Children need to have time out with their friends, so plan ahead for them to have friends over or to go visiting. Although guidelines need to be set for the duration of time spent with friends, be flexible so your children don't feel hemmed in.
8. Encourage your children to attend study groups to enhance their school work. If the school doesn't have them, encourage your children to form their own with their close friends.
9. When children are studying extra hard, for instance at exam time, offer them incentives for hard work done. Take them to the movies or out for dinner. They need time to relax. They also need encouragement and support.

Problems at school

When your children leave home of a morning, or you drop them off at school, they have a long day ahead. Your children's outlook or attitude at the beginning of the day can affect how they perform in their school work. If there are pressures, arguments or unhappiness at home let your children's teachers know. They may be able to look out for telltale signs that your children are suffering at school and offer some help.

Take notice of what your children are like when they come home. If they are having problems at school with friends or teachers, or having difficulties with their subjects, then it is important to get onto the problem straight away. One of my daughters had a personality clash with her teacher. At the time I felt we could get through it by talking it through together and I explained that not everyone can get on. We tried to put the differences and problems she was having aside by acknowledging them, but the problems got worse. My daughter wasn't doing any school work at all and eventually ran away from school. After a lot of tears and heartache I finally did something about it. I simply changed my daughter's school, sending her to a school that I felt was best suited to her character. Now, as soon as a problem arises, I go straight to the teacher and we sort out any problems as quickly and as amicably as possible. Remember, children are living in stressful times and the quicker we can help them get over these hurdles, the better.

Exams

Dare anyone mention the final year exams? In their final years at school, teenagers lead a very stressful life—intermingled for many of them with a heavy social life of party after party!

Many parents have a tough time coping too—loaded with anxiety, hoping and praying that their son or daughter will get the marks they need to go on to further study or get the job they want. Final year exams are a time of letting go for parents and allowing teenagers to work at their own pace. I told my son I was there to support him in whatever he did as long as he felt comfortable about what he was doing. Some students study for exams, others leave their studying until the last moment. Many final-year students become highly emotional. They suffer from anxiety, sicknesses, insomnia, poor eating habits and so on. As parents, all we can do is offer support and an ongoing routine to help them feel as secure and safe as possible.

School reports

School reports are just an indication of how your children are doing at school. Even if the marks are not what you expected, look at the effort marks. You may have been very good at one subject but your children may be good at something else. Encourage your children in their work. If your children need strengthening in certain subjects, it is best to discuss with their teacher where and how your children can be helped.

One further piece of advice: school reports are funny things and many parents want to know if their children have done better or worse than other children in the class. Sharing information with other parents or children can be detrimental to your own children. Parents who are competitive may want their children to outdo your children any way they can. Often comments are made to their children that get passed on to your children, which can cause awkward situations or feelings of hurt and resentment. Swapping school reports is not a good idea. They are only to be used as a guideline for how to improve on or continue doing well in their school work.

Signs to look for if your children are not coping at school

1. Anxiety attacks: nervousness, fearfulness, wetting the bed, and lacking confidence are all signs of anxiety attacks.
2. Sudden changes in eating and sleeping habits.
3. Not wanting to go to school or using delaying tactics, not starting or completing tasks.
4. Introverted or extroverted behaviour that is out of character, for instance being too quiet or very loud verbally.
5. Rushed homework: that is, not spending the usual amount of time on homework, or not putting in the usual effort.
6. Not mixing with their usual friends.
7. Ongoing sicknesses, for instance stomach aches or headaches without a proven medical condition.

Successful learning

Positive sayings to help build your children's educational skills

- I am able to concentrate clearly and effectively, taking in and retaining all the relevant information I need for my highest success.
- I am a clever, intelligent person.
- I read and write with ease.
- I am calm and relaxed in all situations especially in tests and exams.

Learning's a breeze

A meditation to help your children learn to the best of their ability

Sit comfortably in a chair with your back straight. Now close your eyes. As you do, take a deep, long, slow breath in. Hold it, then let it go with as much force and strength as you can; feeling the breath leave your body. Do that two more times and feel your body relax. Now think about your left arm; feel it, imagine it becoming light and free. Now think about your right arm; feel it, imagine it becoming light and free. Feel your chest area; your rib cage moving as you breathe in and out. Let the sensation in your chest become light, airy and free. Now relax your left leg all the way down to your toes. Gradually allow your left leg to become light and free. Let go of all sensation from your left leg. Now relax your right leg, all the way down to your toes. Feel it getting lighter and lighter, and let all sensation go. Your whole body feels light, airy and free. Notice how you are feeling. Now direct your thoughts to your head and face. Feel and sense your head and face. Relax your head and neck by taking another deep breath in and out. Feel your eyes relax, your nose relax, and your mouth melt into the air that surrounds and calms you. You are now in a very relaxed state of mind. Acknowledge any thoughts or feelings that come to you and let them go.

As you sit quietly, imagine you are sitting on a deserted beach. Your mind is clear and you are calm and relaxed. Feel the sand supporting your body. Feel the air brush past your face. The sky above you is clear and blue; there is not a cloud to be seen. Now look out in front of you to where the waves of the deep blue sea are crashing down hard upon the shore. Let yourself become part of the waves. Feel all your fears, worries and tensions disappear as you ride each wave.

When you have let go of all negative thoughts, feelings and emotions bring yourself back onto the shore and sit peacefully with a clear mind. Know now that your mind can receive any information when it wants. You only have to ask. Take the time now to ask of the universe anything that you desire. Listen for its reply.

When you feel you have had enough time on this beach stand up and start walking to the exit ramp. As you do, know that you have clarity and knowledge at your fingertips. Sense how you feel as you walk up the exit ramp with ease and determination. This is who you are. When you are ready open your eyes, reach for a piece of paper and write down all your thoughts about your journey. Now you know you can achieve all you set out to do, and that you can always take the time to sit on your beach when you are stressed or anxious to release and let go.

Suggested Australian Bush Flower Essences

To relieve anxiety: Dog Rose, Crowea
To treat bed wetting: Red Helmet, Dog Rose
To combat depression: Kapok Bush, Flannel Flower, Wild Potato Bush, Red Grevillea
To treat dyslexia: Bush Fuchsia, Sundew, Jacaranda
To alleviate headaches: Emergency Essence, Five Corners, Paw Paw, Sturt Desert Rose
To reduce insomnia: Black-eyed Susan, Crowea, Boronia
To reduce nervousness and restore calm: Dog Rose, Black-eyed Susan, Jacaranda

Parents' page

Educating your children

It will be hard to accept at first, but you must understand that your children are going to take their own path eventually. You can only guide them and support them to the best of your ability. Here are a few tips to help you educate your children:

1. Try to relax and allow your children to grow with help from their school and yourself.
2. Try not to impose your dreams and wishes on your children.
3. Support your children in whatever they do, even if you don't always agree with their choices.
4. For your own sanity and your children's, keep their routines going.

Positive thinking and self-confidence will help your children succeed through their school years. Encourage them to use their journals daily to keep track of how they are going. Help them to say their affirmations and prayers daily to keep them spiritually educated. If they get tense, the occasional warm bubble bath or massage will help relieve tension. Incorporate these with Australian Bush Flower Essences to help release any ailments that occur. Finally, encourage your children to meditate regularly especially just before studying and before exams. It will help them to focus their thoughts and energies on their work. Meditation before going to bed will help them get a relaxed night's sleep and be healthy in mind, body and spirit the next day, enabling them to absorb what they are being taught.

Positive parenting—sayings to help you guide and support your children

- I am a good parent.
- I am being supported and am supporting those around me in a calm and collected manner at all times.
- I am able to communicate with my children and their school with clarity and ease.
- I approach any challenges with clarity and ease, achieving a positive outcome at all times.

Flight for freedom—a meditation to help you just relax and be quiet and still

Sit or lie down making yourself really comfortable. Close your eyes. Now, very slowly, take three long breaths in and out. As you take each breath, feel the air pass in and out your body.

Just above you is a golden sun. Feel its rays warm the top of your head. Gradually feel its warmth creep down your body filling every part of you. Just sit or lie in the glow of the warm golden light.

Now, imagine yourself sitting at the top of a very high cliff overlooking the sea. The sky is blue and the earth beneath you is green with luscious, soft grass. You are surrounded by beauty and colour. Looking out, you see a ship on the distant horizon, bobbing up and down on the gentle waves. The motion of the ship and the waves make you more and more relaxed. There are people on the boat laughing and shouting, calling to you to join them, but you know this time is for you and you alone. A precious time. A gift for you. You remain seated calmly and are totally relaxed, watching the ship pass you by. A bird glides on a current of wind in front of you. As you watch the bird glide aimlessly in the clear blue sky, you feel yourself emerge as one with the bird. A sense of freedom and weightlessness washes over you. As you glide on the wind, let go of any thoughts, feelings or worries you may have. Watch them drift away on the breeze and let go.

Feel yourself gently come to settle once more on the green, luscious grass. Know now, you are totally supported by all of nature's gifts. You are calm and relaxed in all you think, say and do. Know that if another ship full of people should come your way you can cope with whatever situation they may present to you. You will know what to think, say or do in a relaxed, confident manner.

When you are ready open your eyes and have a great big stretch. Acknowledge how you feel and know that in any stressful situation you can come back to your place at the top of the cliff, and soar on nature's path to peace and serenity.

Suggested Australian Bush Flower Essences

To relieve anxiety: Dog Rose, Crowea
To combat depression: Kapok Bush, Flannel Flower, Wild Potato Bush, Red Grevillea
To alleviate headaches: Emergency Essence, Five Corners, Paw Paw, Sturt Desert Rose
To reduce nervousness and restore calm: Dog Rose, Black-eyed Susan, Jacaranda

Now you have discovered ways to help your children learn skills needed for success, but they also need other people in their lives. Friends are very important and, although we only make and keep a limited number of friends throughout our lives, many people cross our path.

3
FRIENDSHIPS AND THE OPPOSITE SEX

Friendships link souls to share a moment in time to grow and flourish.

In the previous chapter we discovered ways to help our children learn and grow but they cannot grow without input from others in their lives. How our children feel about themselves at any given time can determine the sort of friendships they make.

Children with high self-esteem are more likely to draw people and situations to them that are good for them. You must bear in mind that most teenagers will experience drugs, cigarettes or alcohol at some stage while they are growing up. But children with poor self-esteem will put up with situations and behaviour from their peers that is not acceptable. They may even go into relationships to sabotage their own success because they don't believe they deserve any better. They compromise their integrity just to be or feel liked. These children are sometimes shy and withdrawn, or they go over the top with their behaviour trying to impress. They have difficulty making friends and may find it difficult to join in conversation, or they brag and are outcasts because of their silly behaviour. By helping your children to realise their good points, you help boost their morale and give them the necessary confidence to stand up for themselves and their beliefs.

You can't like all your children's friends but if you encourage your children to bring their friends home and make them welcome, at least you will know where your children are and with whom.

A recipe—how to choose and be a good friend

Mix together a large cup of everything.

Ingredients

1. Accept and love yourself for who you are
2. Respect each other
3. Trust each other
4. Share common interests
5. Share similar values and outlooks on life
6. Do your own thing or be together
7. Be honest and open
8. Have fun
9. Be flexible
10. Have good communication and listening skills
11. Be able to share and keep secrets
12. Be reliable
13. Show encouragement and supportiveness through thick and thin

The playground bully

He or she stands out a mile—the playground bully. According to Bullying Online, bullying occurs in every school but it is how we deal with it that makes the difference. Being the victim of bullying can cause loss of sleep, a sense of living in fear, not eating properly, staying away from school, depression and so on; all because your children are unable to stand up for their own feelings and rights, for fear of recrimination. The playground bully walks the path that can lead some children to take drastic actions, often acting out of character, and many children suffer from depression as a result. Children who are bullied feel degraded and their lack of self-worth becomes too much to bear. In such severe cases I recommend contacting Bullying Online for assistance. The website is listed at the back of the book. You may also need to take your children to see their doctor so that the problem can be recorded properly.

Children bully in many different ways: for example, name calling, gossiping, saying nasty things about someone in their presence, threatening others, repeatedly leaving a member out of team games and so on. Boys tend to physically abuse each other, whereas girls tend to be bitchy using ridicule and name calling or excluding their victims from group activities.

Bullies tend to be children who seek attention. They are strong characters who are able to draw weaker characters around them by using force, but their highly aggressive manner is often a cover for the hurt they have endured through lack of love and attention, or through physical abuse. A bully has learnt they can get what they want through violent and aggressive behaviour. Sometimes these children are jealous of another child or just want to look important. Many bullies don't even realise what it is like to be bullied and never understand how their victims feel.

It's sad, but the only thing many of these kids want is love and attention. Many of them respond quite differently when given responsibilities with animals or younger children, showing their kinder, softer nature. Such situations reach an inner part of their soul connecting them with nature. Although the bully does not like being seen as soft, softness is what they need.

Standing up to bullies

How do we teach our children to stand up to bullies? There are certain tactics that can be used without drawing more attention to the situation. Telling on the playground bully doesn't work, it only exacerbates the situation, and the bullies seem to come back with more force. Instead, teach your children to be assertive, not aggressive. Get your children to stay in a group so they cannot be singled out, especially in the playground or on the bus or train to and from home. Encourage your children and their friends to stay near a teacher or authority figure because a bully isn't going to attack anyone under the nose of a teacher.

Work on developing your children's self-esteem so they feel good about themselves. When they are more confident and sure about themselves the school bully will leave them alone.

Phone calls

All children love the phone, especially teenagers who would talk for hours if they could. The telephone is part of a teenager's life and part of their development. Here are some guidelines you may like to implement that will help reduce your present phone bill and still allow your children to develop socially:

1. Set a reasonable time for each phone call (for instance, 10 minutes) and put a clock, watch or timer by the phone so they can see it clearly.
2. Allow your children a set number of phone calls per night.
3. Agree to have no interruptions during homework or study times.
4. Give them some privacy.

5. Take their telephone messages and allow a time for them to return phone calls.
6. Ban national or overseas calls unless they have asked for and received your permission first.
7. If your children want to make longer phone calls then perhaps you can come to some arrangement whereby they pay for their calls.

More than just friends

When children are small they love everyone but when they get to around eight or nine they dislike the opposite sex. As your children grow and develop so do their relationships with others, and that includes relationships with the opposite sex too. Meeting and having a relationship with a member of the opposite sex is quite nerve-racking, especially when your children are still finding out who they are. Can you remember how you felt when you had your first crush? Can you remember the first kiss?

These days girls seem to like well-mannered guys who are gentle and true to themselves. Both males and females enjoy being friends. Many teenagers have very strong views on what is right and wrong especially about things like smoking, alcohol and drugs. Whatever relationships your children make they need to be open and honest. Many emotional games get played and your children have to wade through them. Choosing friends for them or not allowing them to see certain people will not solve anything; it can make things worse. Discussing your children's relationships with them will help build healthy, fruitful relationships. Make your children aware of users and abusers in destructive and heartbreaking relationships. Teaching your children to trust their gut feelings can help them walk away from negative situations when they happen.

When relationships are abusive or are breaking down you

may notice your children or their boyfriends/girlfriends borrow things and do not give them back for a long time, especially after persistent reminders. They may ask to borrow money, always crying poor and never repaying debts, or they may always seem to have a sob story to make you feel sorry for them. They may get others to do things their way or not at all, and they apply pressure sexually when the other person is not ready.

Most children like to go around in groups which makes them feel comfortable, but as they get older they begin to form more serious relationships. Many teenagers experiment with sexual intercourse when they are around 15–16 years of age, the first time is often in the family home. For many, their first sexual experience doesn't live up to their expectations as nerves and lack of experience mar the event, and an alarming percentage of teenagers still do not use contraceptives.

Teach your children to have fun, by making friends, setting sexual boundaries and enjoying the thrill of romance. Their first serious relationship will teach them much about chemistry and intimacy. They will have to learn about trust, commitment, respect, mutual interests, and acceptance of themselves and of their friend. Of course, as a relationship becomes more intense so do the emotions. Falling in love is magic: falling out of love is traumatic.

When the relationship breaks down, there are some vital signs to look for. Children can stay hurt for weeks. Their self-esteem plummets and they moon about hoping their friend will come back. Until a new love comes along! Here are some signs for your children to look out for when their loving relationship is breaking down. Their partner . . .

- doesn't return phone calls
- makes excuses and finds other things to do
- says they've got something to sort out and needs to talk
- changes the way they dress or look

- says they have other friends to see, and is busier more often than usual
- is not so attentive.

If your teenager is breaking off a relationship, advise them to be strong, be honest, and show gratitude for being able to share the other's time and energy. Boys seem to move on quicker than girls, and they seem to have difficulty staying just friends, so be warned.

Relationships with the same sex

Another issue that could really bring your teenagers' self-esteem down is discovering they are gay. As they realise they are gay, they undergo a process of questioning their sexuality; not knowing who to tell, how to deal with keeping their secret, and living in fear of what to do if someone finds out. Their self-esteem plummets and many suffer from severe depression.

One young gay man I know is able to be quite honest and open about his sexuality, but it took a lot of courage to get where he is now. He had come to terms with his sexuality, but not without many years of pain and suffering. When he talked about his mother and father he said they were role-model parents.

'Many of my friends ran away from home as early as 14 and 15, too frightened to go home because of the repercussions, too frightened about the anger that might be expressed,' he said.

He went on to tell me there were three or four boys in his year at school who were always the odd ones out, congregating in one area of the playground. None of them was aware of the other's predicament until they left school. He suffered from severe depression, but his parents helped him cope and have supported him ever since.

When Rick, however, told his parents he was gay, his father couldn't cope with the idea, and after a lot of fighting and arguing his parents' marriage broke up. His mother remarried and her new husband was far more accepting of Rick and made his life more bearable, giving him a family again. If your teenagers can't talk about their sexuality, find someone with whom they can; it may be a counsellor, family friend or a doctor. Ensure that it is someone you both trust. The reference section at the back of the book may help you decide where to go for advice or counselling.

Rejection

Ouch, that hurts! It hurts us all, at any stage of life, but children take rejection very hard. Egos get bruised. Those with high self-esteem pick themselves up and move on to the next encounter, but those with low self-esteem blame themselves. They tend to go over and over in their minds where they went wrong. It is healthy to feel hurt, to feel disappointed and acknowledge these emotions, but it is also healthy to bounce back and start anew. If your children reject another for whatever reason, they must try to not carry the guilt with them.

One young girl, Tanya, broke off a relationship with a friend she had known for only a short time. Tanya and Sara were great mates at school but as soon as they went out in public Sara behaved quite differently compared to when they were alone together. Tanya found herself in embarrassing situations. She felt awkward and out of place. She discovered that Sara was not really someone she wanted to be around away from school. After discussions with her parents Tanya told Sara how she felt. Now Tanya spends time with friends she is more comfortable with, but still acknowledges Sara at school.

Another teenager, Kate, who had been bitten by the love bug, decided that her romance with Ben was over. Ben didn't like the fact that the relationship was over so after her rejection he followed Kate home. As soon as Kate opened the front door of her home, Ben rushed in trying to force her to reconsider her decision. In the process Ben became emotional and over-zealous and hurt Kate. Ben's emotions overrode his sanity because his heart ruled his head. Luckily another member of the family was home to come to Kate's aid, but it took Ben a long time to get over the relationship.

Being rejected in a friendship or courtship can be painful. The best way to recover is to acknowledge the pain and hurt, feel it, then release and let go. Dwelling on it only brings about more pain and any suppressed feelings will rise again later, in another relationship.

Image

Children need to portray their individuality to the world, and establish their own image. This helps to attract certain sorts of people to them and is a very important part of building relationships. Some children have no interest in clothes whatsoever, but image and cleanliness are important. Teaching your children at an early age to love themselves and take pride in their appearance builds their confidence, giving them a winning edge in all they do. Children need to know how to dress accordingly, expressing their own personality. This can be great fun for you too.

My children have always chosen their own clothes but they have certain guidelines. For example, I discuss with them exactly what items are needed. Their clothes should be colour co-ordinated with other items already purchased. They must consider whether the new clothes can be worn with other clothing items; do they fit the budget; are they practical or appropriate for use and so on? This has worked very well for us and allows my children to enjoy the art of wearing clothes that express their age and personality.

It is okay to guide them, but let them make their own final decisions. After all they are going to be the ones wearing the outfit. By asking your children to help choose their clothes you can reduce the amount of clothing left unworn in the cupboard.

Tristan, a little boy I know, was changing schools and on the first day at his new school his mother made him wear a pair of red tartan trousers which he hated. Well, as you can imagine the kids in the class loved them! As Tristan stood in front of the class introducing himself, he heard the children snigger. He couldn't wait to sit down to hide behind his desk and the end-of-school bell didn't come fast enough. After school he raced home and hid the trousers in a very dark place.

What you like may not be to your children's taste so you may have to compromise. If they feel comfortable in their outer clothing their inner being will shine through.

Hygiene

Personal hygiene is terribly important. Teenage boys seem to think they'll dissolve if water touches them, and girls think the shampoo bottle is really only for decoration.

This is the time to teach them about personal grooming; washing their hair, conditioning it, cutting their nails, using deodorant, cleaning their teeth, changing their clothes regularly and even washing their clothes themselves.

Girls need to be taught about using feminine hygiene products; how to use tampons and pads, store them and dispose of them. Make sure they have some with them at all times in case of an emergency. They need to know the importance of changing them regularly and keeping their bodies clean.

Teach your children from an early age to take care of their bodies; cleanliness is a beautiful thing.

Dressed to express

There are so many beautiful clothes available for children, all suiting different needs and budgets. All my children are different in their dress preferences which is frustrating when trying to pass clothing down. My eldest daughter likes dressing up with fancy clothes and shoes. My son loves shorts, T-shirt and jeans. My other daughter likes baggy clothing. Well, each to their own. But each child takes pride in how they look. With so many different fashions around, children are able to choose clothes to suit their personality. One thing seems absolutely common among teenagers—they love to wear black.

First impressions

We live in a society where first impressions are important. Some people will think differently about us because they have pre-conceived ideas about who we are from what we wear. That's why it's a good idea to teach children at an early age how to present themselves according to situations and circumstances while still expressing their individuality. All children need to understand there is a time and a place for everything; so turning up in scruffy jeans to a job interview or an oral exam could be inappropriate.

Each generation goes through its own phases and fashions for clothing. When I look back at some of the outrageous things I wore as a teenager I realise I must have looked a sight but I was having fun. I'll never forget the outfit I wore to a dance at our church social with my best girlfriend when I was fourteen. The band played 'My Sweet Lord' all night. Hot pants were in and I wasn't allowed a pair, so my girlfriend and I improvised. We spent hours sewing purple felt braces onto an old pair of white shorts and glued purple hand-shapes on the bottom. My hair was curled into a mass of frizzy curls.

Then we hit the dance floor. What a sight! But it was off with the makeup and back into my 'straight' clothes before I went home.

Beautiful friendships

Positive sayings to help your child be a good friend and attract good friendships

- I am a beautiful person with many wonderful friends. I am a true friend to my friends.
- My body is beautiful and I attract the right people to me at all times.
- My relationships with others are honest, loving, caring and positive.
- I am confident when I meet and speak with other people, especially with the opposite sex.
- I always have fun with my friends and even when things seem to go wrong we are able to sort out our differences quickly and positively.

Life's train ride

A meditation to help your children build healthy relationships with those around them

Lie or sit down and get really comfortable. As you lie quiet and still, I want you to take three deep breaths. As you do this, I want you to become aware of your head and face. Screw your face up tight and then relax each and every muscle. Relax. Now focus on your neck and shoulders. Tense every muscle and then let go. Relax. Tighten every muscle in your left arm and clench your fist. Now relax, feeling each muscle release and let go. Concentrating on your right arm tighten all the muscles and let go. Feel your head, neck, shoulders and arms sink deeper and deeper. Feel yourself become heavy. Now take a deep breath and tighten your chest, stomach and abdomen muscles. Hold them, and then let go. Turn your focus now to your left leg and foot, tightening all the muscles and then letting go. Now do the same with your right leg and foot. As you lie or sit here notice that you are totally relaxed. You are also intensely aware of your body.

You are now going on a journey in a train. Imagine yourself standing on the platform of a station as the train draws in. Open the door and choose a seat, one that you feel comfortable sitting in. As you look around, you see all the people you know in your life. Some you like or love and some you don't. Stand up and face all these people. If there is anyone on your train that is not here to help, love, care and support you in your life's journey you must ask them to leave the train now. Just watch who gets up and leaves. When these people have gone, your train starts to move and sets off in a direction that is best for you. How fast is the train going? Do you want to get to your new destination quickly or are you looking out the window enjoying your journey? Ask yourself why you are travelling in such a way and wait for the answer.

You arrive at the next stop and as you sit there new people get on your train. These are all the people coming into your life to help you on your life's journey. Say hello to them and send them love. Have a look at them. Trust that you are going the right way now. If you need help ask these people to help you. They love you for who you are. You can feel their love all around you. Soak it all up. You are a wonderful person and you are confident in all you say and do. You dress the way you want and people can see the real you. Your beauty shines out.

When you are ready open your eyes and have a great big stretch. Be aware of who you are. Give yourself a great big hug and tell yourself that you love yourself.

Suggested Australian Bush Flower Essences

To treat acne: Spinifex, Five Corners, Billy Goat Plum
To relieve anxiety: Dog Rose, Crowea
To reduce body odour: Dog Rose, Five Corners, Billy Goat Plum
To improve the nails: Fringed Violet
To reduce nervousness and restore calm: Dog Rose, Black-eyed Susan, Jacaranda
To reduce stuttering: Five Corners, Bush Fuchsia, Dog Rose

Parents' page

As a parent you cannot choose your children's friends. You can only guide them and hope they will remember all the things you have taught them, especially the core family values. I have banned two children from my household over the years because their behaviour was really bad. When other children enter your house they have to abide by the rules of your home. If they cannot accept that, then their only option is not to come at all.

When your children begin to build loving relationships the best you can do is to catch them when they fall. You cannot save them from the occasional broken heart. Broken hearts vary in degree of pain, as you know, but you can only support and help them in a way that they feel comfortable with. My son never wanted to tell me about his first kiss because he thought I would laugh and make fun of it, whereas, when I found out, I thought how wonderful it was. I must admit, when I met the young lady in question my breath was taken away. She was tall, blonde and voluptuous. I couldn't believe she was really my little boy's girlfriend.

Growing up

When children discover they are attractive to the opposite sex a whole new world opens up to them. With my daughter,

I noticed how all of a sudden her appearance was frightfully important. All the preening and hours spent in the bathroom were and still are outrageous. It is up to us to prepare our children for these relationships, educating them in all areas, especially sex. Let them know that they can talk to you freely about any problems or challenges they may encounter but try not to pry. This is their path of discovery, one of growing up.

Personally I find Kinergetics very effective in sorting out relationship troubles. We all play out our roles in life and many of us repeat old patterns over and over again. Kinergy seems to help us break these cycles and find other ways of dealing with situations as they arise. I think it is important to keep a journal. When new situations arise you can look back through your journal to see how you dealt with the situation last time. Then you can decide how to approach the situation this time around. Prayer and meditation will also help solve any niggling doubts, giving you clarity and helping you focus on which direction to take.

Building positive relationships—positive sayings to help you in your relationships

- I attract all the relationships and situations I need to help me achieve my mission in life.
- I trust my children with all my heart and soul, and know they draw to them the relationships they need for their highest good.
- My self-image is the real me. The real me shines through for everyone to see and I am happy with who I am.
- I am supportive, loving and caring at all times.

Layer by layer—a meditation to help you look at your inner self and the image you want to portray

The image that you portray and see is your mirror in the world so take pride in yourself, and be confident in what you do and say, and your children will mirror you.

Lie down and get comfortable. Take a long deep breath. As you breathe, you breathe in a wonderful white light. As you breathe out let go of anything that is worrying you. Take another long, slow, deep breath in, filling your whole body with this beautiful white light. Feel the white light fill every part of you and then imagine the light pouring out every pore of your skin. You are now shining like a beacon for all to see.

Now I want you to see yourself peeling away a layer of your skin as though you are peeling an onion. Then peel another layer, and another, until you feel you have reached the innermost core of you. When you reach your core, look at yourself. Ask who you are and listen for the reply. Are you happy with who you are? If not, ask what you can do to change. Listen for the reply. When you have listened to what is being said, gently draw each layer of skin back into place and seal it with love.

Imagine yourself standing in front of a long mirror. Look at the person standing before the mirror. This is you, the real you. Your light is still shining through. Acknowledge who you are. Send love to the image standing in the mirror. You are a beautiful human being. Everything you do is right for you and those around you. Know now you draw all the people around you that you need for your highest purpose. Let go of anyone you feel may be hindering you. As you stand in front of this mirror ask yourself to be true to you. There is no one else like you in the world. When you decide to open your eyes, know that you are here to make your mark. You are who you are, because you love who you are. Know that even if you stumble and fall and don't always live up to your image, you will be picked up and helped along the way. You have people around you who love and care for you; let them see your beacon shining and be proud of who you are.

Suggested Australian Bush Flower Essences

To relieve anxiety: Dog Rose, Crowea

We have looked at how to educate your children; helping them to develop their life skills, how to present themselves to the world, and how to make friends and build healthy relationships. But how should they behave? Where do they get their traits? In the next chapter, I discuss how you can help your children develop behavioural skills that are acceptable in our society.

4
BEHAVIOUR

> We each have a purpose in life and our individuality makes each one of us special and unique.

Good, bad, healthy and unhealthy

In earlier chapters we focused on you, the parent, and how you can educate and develop your children with the help of others around them. Now we are going to look at how your children behave in different situations.

Our children are reflections of ourselves. They look to us to set an example. According to the Australian Institute of Professional Counselling, children inherit 25 per cent of their parents' traits and 12.5 per cent from each of their grandparents. They learn many of their attitudes from us, and develop others through the culture they are raised in, their peers, religious background, school, the media, and so on. While we have an amount of control over our environment, it is important to understand that we can only have full control over ourselves and not our children. As parents we can guide our children, but only they can make changes in their own lives. If your children want to make changes in their lives they need to identify the changes they want to make at this time; acknowledge their desire for change; find the motivation to make the change, and take action.

Children have their own specific needs and desires and these need to be acknowledged and satisfied if they are to lead healthy, successful lives with high self-esteem. When these needs are not met, or are suppressed, they may experience stress, inner conflict or frustration, which in turn may affect your children's mental, physical and emotional health.

Your children's attitude towards life is learned behaviour, formed by life experience. They are constantly assessing, judging and modifying their attitudes consciously and subconsciously. When they are presented with a new situation their attitude either reinforces an existing belief, forms a new attitude, or upgrades an old one. Your children's personality and their attitudes form the way they behave. To create a balance, it is important that the flow between their personality (their emotions, feelings and instincts) and their attitudes (their learned behaviour) is constant and consistent. Bear in mind though that attitudes manage our personalities and sometimes your children's attitudes will override their instincts.

As parents, we must help our children identify their needs and desires so they may realise their dreams. We must also help them identify which attitudes and what behaviour is appropriate in their environment. With the right guidance, children quickly learn what sort of behaviour is sociably acceptable.

Children have very basic needs like love, support, safety, food and shelter. When children's basic needs are not met they lose self-esteem. Their behaviour deteriorates and the cycle begins. When your children behave in a way that is unacceptable, it is important you help them find ways to change their attitudes which will change their behaviour. First you need to find out what caused the upset and deal with it.

All children play up—none are angels. They are constantly testing you to see how far they can go. They want to see how you will react. Your reaction is the example they will learn from.

I believe in a reward system for children. Some parents call it bribery but I believe we all need to have a carrot dangled in front of our eyes sometimes. It gives us motivation and that is a very powerful tool. If your children perform well, I believe they should be allowed to gain something for it. For example, you might offer your children 50p a day to make their bed, or allow them to order lunch from the school canteen if their room is kept tidy four days in a row.

Recently, at a counselling seminar I went to, a nanny mentioned that she had offered a reward system to her charges but they turned to her and said, 'You're bribing us.' The nanny pointed out that she was being rewarded or bribed weekly by being paid to look after them. We all like some reward, or incentive, that little bit of extra motivation; especially for something we really don't like doing.

Effective communication skills

Better communication is the key to helping your children learn more about themselves and for learning healthy attitudes. Teach your children to ask questions. As teenagers, teach them the art of negotiation. Teach your children to look at the options, the pros and cons, get them to use their brains. Guide them into making their own decisions. Get them to evaluate situations and help them take responsibility for their decisions. If they are frightened, help them release their fear by getting them to realise and acknowledge their personal obstacles. As you teach your children to get in touch with themselves, be careful not to lead them or impose your own expectations on them.

Cause and effect

Remember your children may respond differently at different times in their lives. This is because they are constantly reviewing and modifying their lives as they grow older. As life throws up challenges for your children they will react accordingly. You cannot protect them but you can help them to change the way they act, react and interact through their behaviour. To do this it is important for each one of you to know the core values of the family. The following is an exercise to help you identify the basic values that drive your family.

Parents' page

Family values exercise

How would you describe your family's value system? Write down what you believe your value system is and how your family fits into it, then share it with your family.

Religious and spiritual beliefs
Self:
Family:
What can you do to enhance your family's religious/spiritual beliefs?

Discipline
Self:
Family:
Is the discipline at home being backed by other adults or teachers at school?

Education
Self:
Family:
Is your children's education enhancing their talents and helping them meet challenges?

Goals
Self:
Family:
Are your expectations of your personal goals and those of your family realistic? Are you achieving your goals or imposing them on your children? What do your children want for their lives?

Respect for others and material goods
Self:
Family:
Do the members of your family respect each other? How much emphasis is put on material wealth?

Friends and associates
Self:
Family:
Are your children attracting the people they need in their lives as inter-dependent relationships or co-dependent ones?

Abundance
Self:
Family:
Do you feel you deserve the very best in life? Do your children?

Language
Self:
Family:
Are you and your children conversing in a positive manner, both verbally and in body language? Is there respect in the way you talk to one another?

You must remember to be flexible and adapt to change, but your core values are the basis for all you and your family do.

De-stressing facts

Remember that if one person is stressed over another's behaviour in your household, then everyone is stressed to some degree. If you don't address it you'll experience family breakdown. Did you know that according to a recent study recorded at Sydney University the second highest stress factor in Australia is children's behaviour; the fifth highest is trying to communicate with your children; the ninth is insufficient family time; and the tenth highest is an over-committed family agenda? In my experience three of these factors are time-management related and it is important for you to look at your schedule to assess if you are:

- taking time out for yourself
- giving quality time to both your spouse and your family
- trying to be a super person; trying to be everything to everyone
- communicating, relating, and fulfilling your needs and desires
- guiding your children, not controlling them, and aiding their self-development.

When your children are young you need to show them that:

- they are loved, cared for and supported.
- they can get to know themselves, nurturing their assets and changing their faults.
- they may ask questions and get answers that satisfy their curiosity.
- they can learn organisational skills in all areas of life—at home, in school, on the bus, shopping with mum, in the car, and so on.
- they should take responsibility for their actions, for instance by not blaming everything and everyone else for what happens to them.

- they can join in family meetings or discussions, have their point of view respected and consider themselves a valued family member.

As teenagers your children need to:

- know they can ask for help at any time.
- know they can make their own decisions.
- know how to make, keep and expand friendships.
- learn how to deal with rejection.
- keep in touch with their feelings and emotions.
- feel respected in the way they are spoken to even if their attitude is wrong.
- have privacy.
- feel they are trusted.
- develop by giving themselves direction and setting goals they can achieve.
- keep communication open between you.

In the chapters that follow I have gone into more detail about various emotions and states your children may experience. I have also given examples of some of the appropriate alternative therapies you can use to deal with these situations as they arise. So remember to allow your children the satisfaction of working through life's challenges. There are no real rights and wrongs in life, only our perceptions, and the framework of our society. Allow your children the freedom and the space to be true to themselves and watch them grow with pride.

In the next chapter, we will look at ways of building your children's self-esteem to help them develop confidence, and act in a positive manner in any given circumstance.

5
DEVELOPING SELF-ESTEEM

'It's cool to be different' by Max Dobrochodow (8 years old)

Max suffered from low self-esteem until he was introduced to several alternative therapies, including my meditation tapes. This is the speech he gave to his class and then to his school.

'I believe it's cool to be different for many reasons. I have chosen ten reasons to explain why being different is better than being the same as everyone else.

1. *You stand out in a crowd . . .*
   Some of the good things about standing out in a crowd are that you are easily recognised by people looking for you, you won't be mistaken for someone else and all the people in the crowd can tell you are an individual.
2. *You follow your own beliefs . . .*
   This means you are thinking for yourself and that you only believe in the things you want to believe in, instead of what suits other people.

3. *You look the way you want to look . . .*
   This means being able to wear clothes you like or having your hair the way you like. It also means acting the way you want and doing what you like instead of what other people want you to do.
4. *It shows that you like yourself . . .*
   It is important to like yourself because not everyone is good at everything, so be happy doing the things you can do. Liking yourself helps you deal with people who don't like you. They are allowed to not like you as long as they don't express it in a bad way. If you like yourself you can stand up for yourself better too.
5. *You are more tolerant of other people's feelings . . .*
   By being different you respect the differences in other people. You respect their right to do what they want, wear what they want and think what they want.
6. *You have more confidence in yourself . . .*
   It is important to have confidence for lots of reasons, like standing up in front of lots of people and giving a speech.
7. *It shows others who want to be different that it's okay . . .*
   Lots of people want to be different but worry that others might laugh at them or be nasty to them. If they see someone who is different it might give them the confidence to be different themselves.
8. *You can take responsibility for your own actions . . .*
   This means that you don't have to do what everyone else says and does. No one else can control you. And it means you aren't going to be blamed for other people's mistakes.
9. *You won't get lost in a supermarket . . .*
   Because you are different you will be easily spotted in a busy supermarket, so if you get separated from your parents they'll find you a lot quicker.
10. *There are no two people the same in the world, so everyone is cool . . .*

> If everyone looked and thought the same, everything would be the same; cars, food, drinks and clothes. There would be no Japanese, Thais, Indians, Eskimos, Australians, Europeans, or Americans, which would make the world a very boring place, but it isn't, because everyone is different.

'That's why I believe it's cool to be different—so that everyone has the courage to be themselves.'

We have looked at where children get their behavioural traits from and now we can look at ways to build on these and help your children grow up into healthy successful adults with well-balanced lives. Have you ever heard this type of conversation?

'I'm dumb. I'm stupid. Nobody likes me. I can't do anything right,' the young child whined.

or

'Are you going out tonight?' the parent asked.
'No, I think I'll study,' replied the teenager.
'But everyone you know is going, all your classmates . . .'
'I don't want to go. I've no one to go with anyway.'
'But you never go out, you're always studying. You never bring your friends home.'
The teenager winced.

Medical studies on children with low self-esteem show they suffer from aches and pains, headaches, sleepless nights, mood swings, lack of concentration and loss of memory. They perform badly, cry, get depressed easily, are sensitive, argue over little matters and have great difficulty in making decisions. If this sounds like your child, something needs to be done NOW!

Children and teenagers who suffer from low self-esteem lose their personal power to others easily, putting aside their own morals, values and beliefs. They become depressed, showing signs of stress, lethargy, irritability, and dependence on others and don't have enthusiasm for anything. If your child is like this you must take action IMMEDIATELY!

Children and teenagers with low self-esteem feel they don't fit in. They get rejected by their peers again and again, or compromise themselves dealing with unacceptable behaviour and language just to gain acceptance from their peers.

Does your child seem lonely? Does your child show signs or symptoms of being stressed? Is your child withdrawn around peers, family or others? Children and teenagers with low self-esteem become negative thinkers who blame the world for everything.

Don't wait until it's too late to help your children grow into successful adults. Support them regardless of what happens. Show them you are always loving and caring, offering guidance and support along their life's path.

According to the Centre for Eating Disorders, children who suffer from low self-esteem are more likely to suffer from anorexia nervosa or bulimia. Alternatively, they may turn to drugs or alcohol to hide their hurt and loneliness. Many will suffer from depression.

At some time in their lives, children with low self-esteem will find themselves in a harmful situation they cannot escape. Usually their parents are unaware of what is going on and when they do find out it's too late. The harm is done.

Children with low self-esteem grow into teenagers . . .

Teenagers with low self-esteem grow into adults . . .

Low self-esteem destroys the heart and spirit . . .

Adults with low self-esteem are negative and feel that life has passed them by before their time.

Every child, teenager and adult needs to work on their sense of self-esteem. Children who have high self-esteem are able to pick themselves up after a fall just that bit quicker than children with low self-esteem.

Some parents believe their children have too much self-esteem and why would they need more? For those parents, thank your lucky stars that your children are confident, but remember young people need tender love, care and encouragement to grow into healthy adults. Your children need positive information and encouragement, guidance, tenderness and care. This includes continual reinforcement and reassurance. They can never have too much!

Building life skills

As young children grow into teenagers and then into adults the groundwork you will have given them is very important. Children need to have a framework for their lives and your role as a parent is to provide them with that framework so they can develop their own personalities in a secure, loving environment. The framework is made up of love, support and communication. It is built on your value system as a family. If your children compromise themselves, breaking your or their values, then their self-esteem drops. Sometimes we do things we are not proud of, but we seldom aim for this to happen because we want to be strong enough to stand up for our beliefs.

> Self-knowledge is the beginning of self-improvement.
>
> —Spanish proverb

It is important that your children learn as much about themselves as possible in order to learn what is important for their true, inner selves. Our attitudes seem to change minute by minute, day by day, or week by week as our knowledge expands, but it is important to be aware of who we are in order to deal with life's challenges in a positive, successful way. Reinforcement is the key to building self-esteem especially as children grow into teenagers when self-doubt often becomes an issue.

An exercise for young children's self-esteem

You will need

Relaxation music, paper and coloured pencils.

Activity

Put some nice relaxing music on. On a blank sheet of paper draw a picture of a seed about a third of the way up the page. Ask your children to draw a picture of the seed growing. They should pretend they are the seed, showing how it is growing, or how it would like to grow.

How do your children see themselves growing? Do they have any roots? What do they need to help them grow? How can they be helped in growing up to be a strong plant? What other plants are around them? What colours have they chosen for their plant? Is it a happy plant?

Draw another seed and, again asking them to pretend to be the seed, get them to draw how they would like to be.

How is this different from the previous picture? What can you and your children do to change the way this young seed is growing, so it will grow the way it really wants to?

Communication meltdown

Have you noticed when your self-esteem drops you tend to become miserable, depressed, irritable, and you sabotage yourself until you have pulled yourself out of it? Your children do the same. Their behaviour becomes intolerable because what they really want is someone to take notice of them and to help them stop drowning in their own self-pity. All your positive messages should come with a cuddle, a kiss, a pat on the back and a push as they roll back on track.

There are many reasons why our children's self-esteem drops and some of these include things like:

- feeling constantly criticised at school, at home, by friends or teammates.
- feeling unloved or left out. Perhaps your children do not have enough friends in the playground, or a new baby has arrived at home? Perhaps your work commitments leave no time to spare, or new family relationships have broken old ties?
- feeling controlled or manipulated.
- feeling humiliated or teased in public, in front of other adults or friends.
- feeling they are not succeeding at school work or in sport.
- feeling they are not respected or no one takes any notice of them (especially teenagers when 'nobody, just nobody, understands them!').
- feelings of inadequacy or awkwardness in their appearance. They feel too fat, too thin, have long legs, and so on.

As parents we need to address these issues as soon as they arise to help our children find ways to get out of the doldrums.

Jake

Jake was a young boy I saw recently with a very bad case of low self-esteem, so much so he had almost no confidence left. Jake's school work was awful and always done in triple-fast time. After all, he reasoned, what was the point of really trying if it was going to be wrong anyway. His mother was at her wits' end because he ate to hide his pain. He was constantly teased about his weight and floundered as he tried to run across the soccer field, out of breath, red-faced and sweating. He wet the bed which made him feel low and dirty. His grandparents appeared to favour his sister because she was smart, and she was taken on lots of special trips and holidays, while he was left at home. He even had trouble writing his own name because each time he wrote it he was criticised for his untidy handwriting and slowness. His behaviour got worse and compounded the problem. Finally the crunch came when he stole money from his parents' bedside table. He bought a huge amount of lollies, and took them to the playground to give them to the children he wanted to play with so they would let him join in their games. Jake's mother got a phone call that afternoon from one of the mothers at Jake's school telling her about his behaviour.

Low self-esteem is a bit like quick sand: if you can get help you are okay; if not, like Jake, you can sink fast and may eventually drown.

Teaching them young

Getting your children to know themselves is quite an experience. The more honest they can be the more they discover ways of improving. The positive outcome is that they learn to take responsibility for their own lives, which means they have to learn to modify their behaviour to suit their values and beliefs.

Accepting themselves for who they really are

We are all in search of ourselves; children are no exception. They are trying to become people with vibrant personalities that will be successful at the art of living, so they need to learn from a very early age that being themselves is important. We all come across people in our lives who are living a lie, not just to others but to themselves. Eventually they find living up to others' expectations becomes harder and harder. When they realise they don't like who they are or who they have become, the shock can be quite horrific and their lives can take a self-destructive turn. We need to teach our children that self-love and a pride in oneself are necessities. It is not vanity to love yourself. It is healthy to have an ego as long as it is balanced with a little humble pie. Children have to learn to stand up for their beliefs, be proud of who they are, what they do, and where they come from, because they are wonderful, unique, special people who have the same rights as everyone else. Other children will try to influence your children, shaking their framework to see if they fall apart, but children with healthy self-esteem will make their own choices and be comfortable with them.

We are all winners

To gain self-value, children need to know they can succeed at something. They don't have to be the best, the brightest, the fastest, the most glamorous, they just need to know they have done the best for themselves. It is sad to see parents who push and push their children, wanting more than their children can give. Their faces drop as the ribbons and awards go to the winners, winners who deserve the accolade, but whom your children may begin to resent and despise. They may feel that they haven't done their best and shy away from mum or dad, afraid they will get a lecture on how they could have won if only . . .

Children know if they have given something their full and best attention. They put themselves down if they have not succeeded in the way they had hoped. They don't need the added pressures and put-downs from others. Under this constant barrage of criticism, some children withdraw from an activity because they have already decided the outcome, 'I'm useless, a failure, not good enough. Hey what's the point?'

All children, big and small, need encouragement to do the very best for themselves. They need a jolly good pat on the back and a few words of congratulations, regardless of the outcome. Acknowledge, encourage and congratulate your children's effort and they will keep on trying for their own personal satisfaction.

It's their responsibility

We are trying to teach the children of today to take more responsibility for their own lives, to earn respect and self-value, and be proud of the things they think, say and do. Giving your children little jobs to do around the home, and trusting them to complete the task to the best of their ability, builds their self-esteem, giving them confidence to expand their horizons in the bigger world. Making the bed, washing the dishes, being responsible for the family pet, putting out the garbage, keeping their rooms tidy, dusting, hoovering and so on, helps teach them the art of living while they help you. They can offer to do some of these things at school, in the community, in their clubs, one on one or in group situations and do the task confidently and assuredly. When the task is completed, acknowledge and congratulate them for a job well done. Give them rewards for jobs done well or let them earn points towards things they want on a grander scale. All these things give them a sense of value. Children need to feel wanted, needed, helpful, a part of a team, but they also need to be seen as individuals.

If the task isn't quite up to the standard you expected—and remember we are talking about children doing a job, not yourself—still acknowledge and congratulate but ask them if they could have done it differently or improved on it somehow. You might even show them how it could be improved in a positive manner, without degrading what they have done. Children like to hear you talk about them when they have done something well. It shows you are proud of them and they have done something worthy.

Answering questions

Children need to ask questions to expand their knowledge and develop their own ideas about life. They need to ask questions to form their own opinions. Our days are busy but it is important to take time to help our children find the answers to their questions. The wonderful thing is that even if you really don't know the answer you can discover the answer together and share the experience, that way you both win. There are times when an answer may be better coming from one person than another, but showing an interest in their curiosity helps them ask more questions, and an inquisitive mind expands its knowledge.

Letting go and trust

Being the eldest of three children I tended to take the world on my shoulders. As a child I felt a conflict between being serious and letting my hair down—letting the child within out—because I was always made an example of. Everything that went wrong seemed to be my fault because I should have known better—I was the eldest! But I had places to go, people to see, goals and dreams to achieve and when I could I left home.

After my own experience as an eldest child, I found it hard letting go of my firstborn. When I look back I have allowed my youngest daughter to do so much more at the age of twelve than I allowed her older brother to do at the same age. A story I often share in my lectures happened when I heard my son and a mate of his (they were eleven years old) talking about going up the hill to play in the park. The other boy was the younger of two children and was allowed to do a lot more than my son. I heard my son say to his mate that he wasn't trusted to go up the road. After the boy went home I explained to my son that it wasn't that I didn't trust him, it was other people and things I was worried about. This incident went around and around in my head for the next few days and finally I decided I had to let him go. I would no longer try to protect him from everything. I sent him on an errand to get some milk from the local shop. Half an hour went by . . . 45 minutes . . . and I was starting to get worried. Should I drive up there? It was only a 15-minute walk there and back, after all. Where was he? No, I must stay put, I decided. I repeated to myself over and over, 'I must trust him to the job at hand.'

For some peace of mind I went to the end of the garden, next to the footpath, and hid in the bushes. After a little while a small figure appeared singing away at the top of his voice, 'happy as Larry', totally oblivious to his mother's anguish. All of a sudden the singing stopped and my son yelled out in his loudest voice for the whole neighbourhood to hear, 'What are you doing in the bushes, Mum?' Mother scurried out of the bushes, redder than berries on a holly bush, and exclaimed, 'Oh, nothing, dear. Just tidying up the bushes.'

Each parent will form different guidelines because of the different experiences they had in their own upbringing. One mother I know felt she was far more lenient than a lot of parents. She hoped her decisions about letting her daughter go out and do things were right. She had given her daughter guidelines and told her she trusted her. Her daughter acts accordingly within those set boundaries. Quite often children set their own boundaries within their parents' guidelines because they mutually respect each other and they have a solid value system. Children have a fairly good idea of what behaviour is acceptable or not and, as I'll discuss later about teenagers, they need flexibility.

Middle children always feel left out. The oldest gets to do things they can't and the youngest seem to get everything their own way. Subsequent children to the eldest child get to do things much sooner and in a much more relaxed environment because the ground has already been tried and tested. A second or middle child needs to know they are still unique and special; they are not just being dragged along for the ride but have their special place in the family too.

The youngest child often stays the baby for the longest but is often older and wiser for his/her years in many respects. They do more than any of the others at the same age because the older ones teach them what they know. All children need special, quality time with their parents, to see to needs that are otherwise imperfectly met by the family. Each child has an important role to play in the family, and each one needs to learn to respect the attributes and special talents of those around them. It is important for children's self-esteem to have respect from and for others in the family. Letting go of your children can be hard, but it is necessary for their growth. Hanging on to your children stunts their personal growth. We can protect them to a certain degree but they must also learn from their mistakes.

Teenagers and self-esteem

What a life of contradictions a teenager is! These wonderful children were sent to terrorise the population of parents. Mission accomplished.

I can say this as I have one, and nearly two, of these delightful creatures in my home. Yes, I'll admit it, I have joined the band of parents with teenagers who wonder which way is up and which way is down, or if there is really any difference.

I'm sure one of my teenagers will tell me because they know everything.

Life has turned upside down for them too. Their faces are covered in spots and their bodies are changing daily. They are confronted with the prospect of being an adult and as they look at their own parents, without the rose-coloured glasses they have been wearing for most of their young lives, they find they have many issues to work through. The pedestal they put their parents on may not be quite as high as it was. They have begun to see their parents in a different light and, because it is a time of rebellion against authority, a stand has to be made.

As parents it is a time when we have to let the reins go and hope for the best. It is time for us to keep the guidelines in force but be flexible. Give them more chances to prove themselves and don't back them into a corner. Teenagers have to deal with their own relationships, heavier school workloads, hormones and physical changes, plus confronting sex and issues with the opposite sex.

Teenage years are full of doubt and insecurities—doubts about themselves, their abilities and worth. They have to look cool and play the part. Many make comments to distract us from what they really feel as they don't want to look dumb or childish. All the clowning around is often a mask to hide insecurities. Building your teenagers' self-esteem is vital.

I'm special

Positive sayings to help boost your children's self-esteem

- I am a beautiful human being. I am love. I am loved. I am supported in all I do and say.
- I feel really good about myself because I am special. There is no one else like me. I am unique.
- I am confident in all I do and say.

- I have the strength and the courage to face anything that appears to be difficult or frightening. I know I am always being helped along my life's journey.

Me, myself, I

A meditation to help build your children's strength, courage and conviction

I am going to take you on a little journey to help you realise what a very special unique person you are—there is no one else like you and you can never be replaced by anyone or anything.

So lie down and get really comfortable. Gently close your eyes. As you lie here quiet and still imagine a great big golden sun, right above your head. Rays of sunlight stream down on the top of your head. The rays of golden sunlight spread down through your head and across your shoulders. As the sunlight warms you, you feel safe and comfortable becoming more and more relaxed. The golden light flows down from your shoulders, all the way down your arms, down to each and every one of your precious little fingers. See the golden light sparkle and shimmer. The warmth fills you as the golden light flows gently down through your body, all the way down, through your legs, down to each and everyone of your precious little toes.

Your whole body is golden and it shines so brightly everyone can see how gorgeous you are.

Now imagine you are walking along a path. How does the ground feel? How are you walking? As you walk along try to relax and let go of anything that is worrying or frightening you. Feel the air against your face and the sun warming your body. Listen to the birds in the trees as they sing, welcoming you. Butterflies flutter all around, flitting from flower to flower. Bees buzz, darting from one place to another busily making their honey. Suddenly a little man jumps out in front of you. Have a look at him. He is dressed very oddly but brightly. He looks kind and has a big smile on his face. 'Hello,' he greets you, 'I am here to help you climb that mountain up ahead. Come with me, I'll show you the best way.' He laughs and chuckles to himself as he scurries along the path. You follow him. You see the pathway becoming smaller and smaller; branches from the bushes tower over the path, the ground seems rockier than before. As you continue along the path the little man waves his arms around and as he does the bushes move back and the pathway widens. The ground levels out and you feel safer as you take each step.

The path goes up the mountainside and you can feel your legs getting tired. The little man turns round and throws thousands of little sprinkles at you and all of a sudden you feel as light as air. You feel as though you are floating but you notice you still have your feet firmly on the ground. You are climbing the mountain with the greatest of ease, and finally you reach the top. You look out from the top of the mountain and can see everywhere. The little man leaves you for a moment while you look at the beautiful world all around you. You are a part of this beautiful vision. The little man comes back to your side and with him is a great big lion, his magnificent mane blowing in the gentle breeze. The lion speaks to you.

'I give you the gift of strength and courage. You may use this gift at any time. You now know you are a confident person with a very special job to do here on earth.'

Suddenly a beautiful elegant giraffe appears by the lion's side.

'I give you a gift—the knowledge of beauty—now you understand you are wonderful, clever and beautiful,' says the giraffe.

Finally, a chattering monkey swings down from some branches nearby. He speaks to you loudly and clearly.

'I give you the gift of speech. Now you always speak clearly and positively and everyone listens to what you say,' the monkey says. He darts around and swings back into the trees.

The little man tells you he is going to leave you with the eagles flying around you. Grab one of their wings and imagine yourself flying with them. You are a free spirit and you are being taken where you need to go for your best interests.

When you are ready, I want you to open your eyes and know you have the strength, courage, beauty, uniqueness and confidence to speak out when you wish to be heard. You are special. You are loved by all the creatures in the universe, big and small. You can call on any one of them and ask for help. All you have to do is meditate, ask for the animal you want to talk to and ask them for help. Then listen to what they say.

Suggested Australian Bush Flower Essences

To overcome addictions: Bottlebrush, Waratah, Red Lily, Sundew, Flannel Flower, Five Corners

To deal with anorexia: Five Corners, Dagger Hakea, Grey Spider Flower

To relieve anxiety: Dog Rose, Crowea

To ease asthma: Bluebell, Red Grevillea, Tall Yellow Top, Grey Spider Flower

To restore balance: Jacaranda, Bush Fuchsia, Crowea

To alleviate body odour: Dog Rose, Five Corners, Billy Goat Plum

To deal with bulimia: Billy Goat Plum, Grey Spider Flower, Five Corners

To overcome depression: Kapok Bush, Flannel Flower, Wild Potato Bush, Red Grevillea

To release frustration: Old Man Banksia, Black-eyed Susan, Jacaranda, Sunshine Wattle, Red Grevillea

To ease nausea: Dog Rose, Paw Paw

To overcome nervousness: Dog Rose, Black-eyed Susan, Jacaranda

To deal with being overweight: Old Man Banksia, Wild Potato Bush, Mulla Mulla, Dog Rose, Fringed Violet

To heal pimples: Five Corners, Billy Goat Plum
To help correct round shoulders: Waratah, Dog Rose, Five Corners, Sunshine Wattle
To ease stuttering: Five Corners, Bush Fuchsia, Dog Rose

Parents' page

As we discussed before, it is important to talk with your teenagers to find out what is going on in their lives and find out how they feel. It is not always easy. Encourage them to talk to you about everything. Let them know your door is always open regardless of what is going on in their lives and that you love and support them always.

Encourage your children to find ways of building their self-esteem. Self-development is very important for your children and for yourself. If your children have low self-esteem and you are not coping with their behaviour, professional help may be necessary. Every little bit helps when it comes to building your children's confidence. There are many good books they can read and I have included a list of titles at the back of the book you might like to start with. There are also many self-esteem courses to try.

Encourage your children to mix with people who are good for their self-esteem; people who encourage them in what they do. Compliments and heartfelt comments can also boost their self-esteem so speak to them in a positive way, guiding them when they need it. But remember you cannot live life for them and making decisions themselves gives them more confidence. Build their inner strength and show them how brightly their little light shines—show them you care—show them how proud you are of them. Hug them, kiss them, show you love them regardless of what they do or say.

I have seen many alternative therapies used to enhance children's self-esteem; especially affirmations, Kinergetics, meditation and Australian Bush Flower Essences. As I explain in more detail in Part Two, affirmations can be printed out and stuck on the wall in strategic places, where you and your children can always see them to affirm within yourselves your needs and desires. So many emotions get aroused when our self-esteem is attacked and the bush flower remedies are excellent for daily use to restore balance to your lives.

I am strength, I am courage—positive sayings to boost your being

- I am a beautiful human being. I am love. I am loved. I give love. I am supported in all I do and say and I support others at times of need.
- I feel good about myself because I am special. There is no one else like me. I am unique.
- I am bringing my family up to the best of my ability. I can overcome any challenges that appear, with confidence and clarity.
- I have the strength and the courage to face anything. I know I am always guided along the right path for my highest purpose.

Bloom and grow—a meditation to help build your self-esteem

Either sit or lie down and get comfortable. As you relax take three deep breaths. As you breathe in, breathe in the air's life and energy. As you breathe out, let go of anything that is worrying you or clouding your thoughts. Now imagine a beautiful, white, shimmering thin film all around you, totally encasing you and protecting you from the outside world. This shimmering film protects you from any negative outside influences.

Imagine you are a tiny little person, as small as a fairy or an elf. Your home is at the centre of a beautiful flower. You can choose any flower you like. At the moment the flower is closed up tight like a bud all around you. The sun starts to shine down on the bush holding your flower and you can feel the petals of your flower opening. Feel the petals unfurl. As they do you feel yourself becoming straighter and stronger. Feel the sun beaming down on you, filling you with its energy. Look at the beautiful colour of your flower. The colour fills you with love and strength. The flower is completely open and you feel at peace and in harmony with nature. Lie down on the petal and soak up the universal power it gives you. Suddenly a little rain falls gently down upon you and all you feel is the gentle caress of the water drops. They massage you and make you feel clean and clear. The shower has gone now and the sun shines down on you again. You have the strength and courage to be and to do whatever you want. When you are ready climb down from your flower and grow to be the real you. As you grow back to normal size, thank yourself for being you. Thank yourself for who you are and what you do. Give yourself a great big hug. You are special and unique. You are a child of the universe.

When you are ready open your eyes and know you have the power within you to achieve all you set out to do. You are proud to be who you are so walk tall and be the real you.

Suggested Australian Bush Flower Essences

To relieve anxiety: Dog Rose, Crowea
To restore balance: Jacaranda, Bush Fuchsia, Crowea
To overcome depression: Kapok Bush, Flannel Flower, Wild Potato Bush, Red Grevillea
To release frustration: Old Man Banksia, Black-eyed Susan, Jacaranda, Sunshine Wattle, Red Grevillea
To end nervousness and discover the calm within: Dog Rose, Black-eyed Susan, Jacaranda

This chapter has given you ideas on how to build your children's and your own self-esteem. Building our self-esteem makes us walk tall and proud, confident and secure in our lives. But we can fall into the trap of depending on others to build our self-esteem rather than doing the work ourselves and taking responsibility for how we act and react. It is vital for you to know your own worth. In the next chapter we move beyond the need for others to affirm our self-esteem and learn how to develop and rely on our own sense of self-worth.

6
WHAT ARE YOU WORTH?

Your soul cannot be weighed, measured or sold. Your soul is special, unique and priceless.

How do you value yourself? How valuable are your family members? Is each one priceless? When everyone in your family has high self-esteem you will all function as a contented family. But what happens when one of you feels worthless, no good, useless?

We all have times when we feel as though we are worthless because we depend on others to make us feel worthy. Dependency is the key. In the family each one of us plays a role which makes it important that we each keep our individuality, not losing ourselves in other people. Relationship interaction is a part of life but we tend to fall into relationships with others that become damaging to ourselves because we don't hold onto our real selves. Sometimes mothers lose themselves in their children, and when their children leave home they feel lost. Often spouses lose themselves in their partners and when the partnership breaks down they feel like an empty shell, as I did after I left my marriage. I made another person my whole life in order for them to achieve what they wanted from life and I forgot about myself.

Realising your personal power and valuing yourself are the keys to making you and your family function as the priceless individuals you are. Our brains work in mysterious ways, storing away all the events that happen within our lives. How we respond to an event or a challenge the first time can determine how we behave when a similar scenario next occurs.

Diana

Diana, a dear friend of mine, had a wonderful, life-altering experience of self-value during a Kinergetic treatment. She was experiencing a major trauma in her life and she felt intensely emotional. Her inner pendulum swung way up high from one side to the other. She had a new man in her life and she was swept off her feet. He was everything Diana had asked for and all was fine for a while. Until all of a sudden the courtship stopped. All she got was what she described as two-minute-noodle phone calls. After two weeks of this Diana was a blithering mess, wondering what she had done wrong, and how, and what was wrong with her. Diana's self-worth plummeted. She began to feel she didn't deserve anything good in her life. She used all the ordinary techniques to try and pull herself out of this dilemma. She gave herself little luxuries, rang her friends and so on, but nothing worked.

Diana's Kinergetic treatment revealed she had experienced four similar situations, the same patterns repeated over and over throughout her life. Obviously she hadn't learnt life's lesson last time. The major breakthrough came when she realised that at one time in her life she believed she had everything she ever dreamed of; a beautiful home, plenty of money, her children in private schools, beautiful designer outfits and the list went on. But her relationship was built on her partner walking out the door on Sunday night and not returning home again until Saturday morning. Upon his return she invariably started an argument with her partner to get the power game back into place. Eventually, the thing that tipped the scales for Diana was that her partner was winning bottles of wine from the airlines because he was the most travelled person for that month. She stopped to ask herself if she was really only worth two bottles of wine. Was she worth only a two-minute-noodle phone call? What had happened to her self-worth?

Knowing your self-worth means knowing who you are and respecting others and their place in your life. Self-worth means letting others know you are a valuable human being—worth your weight in gold. Self-worth means being honest and true to yourself and having people around you who are true and honest with themselves and with you. It means making changes to your lifestyle if there is a conflict between your core values and how you live.

Decision making

It is important for children to know that when they make a decision they can be wrong. Many children won't make decisions because they don't believe their thoughts and feelings are valuable. Children, and especially teenagers, have problems with their self-worth. Sometimes, through lack of self-worth, they feel some of the decisions they have made are not right and they put themselves down.

Lee

Lee was 18 and studying for his final exams at school when he decided he knew best about his study schedule—the when, what and how. But his parents felt differently and were worried by their son's attitude and actions towards his study. They had always been supportive of him, in everything he did, and now all of a sudden their son said he knew best. Every weekend he seemed to be at a party or social gathering.

Every evening there was a string of 'must view' programmes on television, and he was using the telephone too often. Lee's parents began to nag him about his study, but he dug his heels in deeper. He thought he knew best. It caused a lot of tension and arguments in the family. Lee felt his parents didn't trust his judgement and his parents believed Lee was not fulfilling his side of the bargain with his school work. Finally the crunch came and Lee said he would leave home if nobody trusted his judgement. His parents backed off and agreed to let their son do his own thing, still supporting him whenever they were needed.

Lee's final exams came—so did the results. Lee did not tell anyone his results for days. He was not happy with them. When he did tell his parents they were very understanding. He had not achieved the marks he knew he could get. Perhaps he had made the wrong decisions but they were his own. No one blamed him or chastised him for what had happened. The family got together and worked out what Lee's options were with the marks he got and today he is happily studying Business Studies and doing very well.

Even when you think your children have grown up and can lead their own lives they still need love, support, encouragement and positive reinforcement in all they do. Be careful not to throw them out of the nest prematurely. They are making more decisions than ever before and are enjoying the power to make them. They can only learn through trial and error. Then they can make the choice about what to do the next time. They want and need to know they have tried and given it their best shot.

Greg

Greg is 16 years old and still at school. He has plenty of goals and knows exactly what he wants to do and by when. As there are so many things he wants to do he needs to earn some money. He got himself a casual job that allows him the freedom to go out, and save for the car he always wanted. As he approaches his final school exams, Greg is also having to make decisions at school that will shape the rest of his life. His teachers and parents can guide him in those decisions, but ultimately it is up to him what he wants to do and achieve. If anybody else made those decisions for him his self-worth would suffer.

We all make decisions, big and small, and we have three choices: we can deal with it ourselves; we can let someone else make the decision for us; or we can leave it and hope it will either go away or sort itself out on its own. The preferred option, the one to encourage your children to choose, is to face and deal with the issue now. Here are nine ways you can help your children make decisions themselves:

1. Give them non-judgemental guidance.
2. Present them with all the options open to them.
3. Present them with all the possible outcomes.
4. Be honest and open.
5. Help them to get in touch with what they are feeling and express their feelings.
6. Get them to look at how a decision suits them as an individual.
7. Offer them someone else to talk to who will not judge them.
8. Help them take responsibility for their lives.
9. Respect their choices.

Physical things your children can do to enhance their self-worth

1. Volunteer their services within the community, take part in 'Clean Up' campaigns, or visit an old people's home.

2. Get in touch with and learn about nature as much as possible; go hillwalking, go bird watching, go to the zoo, go fishing, or beachcombing. Respect life and look for its beauty.
3. Grow their own vegetable garden. Grow parsley, herbs, tomatoes, carrots, or pot plants.
4. Get in touch with positive groups that encourage growth; the Brownies, Cubs, Scouts, meditation classes, dancing/singing groups, Youth Clubs, self-development groups.
5. Join a sports team and learn about teamwork.
6. Find out what they are good at and what they enjoy, and do it to the best of their ability.
7. Wear the clothes that they feel best in, that make them feel comfortable and suit what they are doing.
8. Be honest with themselves and others without hurting others or themselves.
9. Mix with other children who make them feel good and with whom they can be themselves. They don't have to buy friendship!
10. Get and keep fit.
11. Learn about physical appearance and hygiene. Know what image they want to portray and do it.
12. Take time out for themselves; relax and have a spa, read a book or just sit and daydream.

The real me

Positive sayings to improve your children's self-worth

- I am a wonderful human being and I think highly of myself and the things I do in my life. I respect myself.
- I always make the right decisions for myself at the right time for the situation I am in.

- My life is in perfect harmony and I am getting the very best life has to offer.
- My life is full of excitement, love, support, freedom and truth, now and always.
- I deserve the very best in life now and always.
- I have the courage to face and deal with everything life offers me.
- I am clever. I am worthy and what I say and do is very important.

Power energy pack

A meditation to help your children know and realise how valuable and special they really are

You can lie down or sit up for this meditation, so just get yourself really comfortable. Close your eyes. Remember there is no one else like you in the world and you can never be replaced. Now imagine just above your head a beautiful fountain flowing with water. The sun is shining through the water droplets, sending out rainbows that surround you. Feel the colours sink into your body. See yourself tingle and glow with all these colours. See yourself sparkle!

Imagine you are sitting in the middle of a green field. As you look around, you see blue sky, green grass and a golden sun. Suddenly dozens of colourful butterflies flutter around you, their wings covered with magical dust that they sprinkle on you. This dust is special as it builds up your strength and courage. The butterflies fly away. You notice a toadstool close by and you walk over to look at it. Underneath the toadstool you find little people singing and dancing. They are so happy to see you. Shouts of laughter and joy fill the air as the little people let you know they are glad you are part of this world. One little person stands out in front of the rest and hands you a parcel. As you unwrap it you feel its energy pouring out.

'This is your personal power pack,' says the little person. 'It will keep you going whenever times get tough. We are always here to help, all you have to do is call and we'll be there.'

Rain droplets fall gently from the sky, washing your body of anything that is bad, frightening or worrying. Let the water sink into the ground below you and feel the strength and courage rise within you. You are very special and unique. Tell yourself that now.

When you are ready open your eyes and take a great big stretch. Wiggle your fingers, wiggle your toes. You are now energised, full of love, life and peace.

Suggested Australian Bush Flower Essences

To relieve anxiety: Dog Rose, Crowea
To restore balance: Jacaranda, Bush Fuchsia, Crowea
To aid decision-making: Paw Paw
To relieve depression: Kapok Bush, Flannel Flower, Wild Potato Bush, Red Grevillea
To be less reliant on others: Red Grevillea
To remove indecision: Sundew
To help reduce stuttering: Five Corners, Bush Fuchsia, Dog Rose

Parents' page

You and your family are worthy and valuable. Each one of you has a role to play that will enhance and enrich each other's lives.

Love me regardless of what I do or say

Teenage years remind me of the song 'Nobody likes me. Everybody hates me. I think I'll go and eat worms . . .' As the boys grow bigger than their mums and come face to face with their dads, and dads aren't quite sure what happened to their not-so-little girls, our teenagers still need love, cuddles and affection. Even when they have been rude and revolting they need to know you are there for them. Some boys get embarrassed at mum kissing them in public but they still like to know you care. I hang onto the moments when my big boy throws his arms around me and says, 'I love you, Mum.'

Encourage your children to ask for a cuddle if they feel they need one. Explain to them that because of your busy schedule things like cuddles and hugs can be overlooked, but tell them you are never too busy for that special hug, cuddle or talk. Some teenagers still want to be tucked into bed and there's nothing wrong with that!

Words

The way we speak to our teenagers is crucial. From personal experience I know it can be hard to hold your tongue. Name-calling and put-downs can be extremely damaging. As you know, the average teenager is tough and quite resilient on the outside but on the inside they are soft. Many teenagers are frustrated and angry, but frustration can lead to aggression and violence if not dealt with quickly and openly. Anger can be focused positively into assertiveness. Encourage your teenager to be as honest with their feelings as possible. Help them get in touch with themselves through meditation, time out, and self-help courses.

Privacy

Teenagers need a place to call their own. Their bedroom is their sacred haven, a place where everyone enters at their own risk. (Not just because you might find a few things growing under the bed that weren't there the last time you were allowed in!) They need a place where they can be quiet, play extra-loud music, entertain their friends, study and generally blob out. It is not the place for younger brothers or sisters unless they are invited. Privacy is very important in teenagers' lives and, although it is very tempting to go foraging around, their rooms should be treated as their own kingdom and parents must respect it as such.

Many teenagers start covering themselves up, hiding their changing bodies, while others strut about as if nothing has changed. One 12-year-old had a very painful and embarrassing experience while trying to get undressed for bed behind the sofa. She sat on the floor, to be stung on the bottom by a bee! The poor child had to lie on the diningroom table to have the sting taken out. All in aid of a little privacy.

Positive affirmations can help you and your children build self-worth. Affirmations can make your teenagers stronger and more independent in all they do. Kinergetics can clear any blockages that may be holding you back from performing to the best of your ability. Aromatherapy and Australian Bush Flower Essences can help you and your children focus and find the balance you need.

I love me—positive sayings to help you love who you truly are

- My relationships are loving and caring.
- My thoughts, words and actions are positive and have positive outcomes.
- I respect myself. I support myself. I listen to myself and I love myself. I am who I am.
- I am love.
- I am a beautiful human being on the inside and on the outside.

Acknowledging myself—a meditation to help you realise and acknowledge yourself as a wonderful human being and a very competent parent or guardian

Lie down or sit in an upright position and make yourself comfortable. Close your eyes. Take three long deep breaths. Imagine gentle droplets of rain falling on your head, massaging your scalp. Feel these droplets of soft warm water trickle down your neck, across your shoulders and down through your body. They trickle slowly through your body, all the way down your legs and your toes. As each droplet fills your being it gently massages and caresses you.

Now imagine yourself standing at the top of the highest pinnacle of the world. The fresh air swirls around you, refreshing you and invigorating your heart, mind, body and soul. As it swirls around you, collect all your worries and fears together and direct them to your right hand. Now imagine yourself throwing these worries and fears out into the air. Release and let them go. As you do this, feel yourself becoming stronger and taller, more confident and more vibrant, full of the essence of life.

When you are ready, start to walk down from the pinnacle. You are going down to meet all the people in your life that are here to help you achieve your dreams and goals and support you in times of need. They are also here to acknowledge you as a very special and unique person. They value everything you do in life no matter how great or small. Now notice what the ground is like beneath your feet. How fast are you walking?

As you come towards the base of the pinnacle many people run to meet you, their arms out to greet you. Love pours from their hearts to you and your heart joins with them. You are special. You are unique. You are valuable. All your efforts are being acknowledged here and now.

I am going to leave you here to bask in the love of these people. When you choose to open your eyes, have a good stretch and know that you are a wonderful human being with many talents. Just let them show and flow from you.

Suggested Australian Bush Flower Essences

To restore balance: Jacaranda, Bush Fuchsia, Crowea
To deal with bulimia: Billy Goat Plum, Grey Spider Flower
To alleviate constipation: Bluebell, Bottlebrush, Boronia
To ease nausea: Dog Rose, Paw Paw
To overcome nervousness and restore inner calm: Dog Rose, Black-eyed Susan, Jacaranda
To deal with being overweight: Old Man Banksia, Wild Potato Bush, Mulla Mulla, Dog Rose, Fringed Violet

Once self-esteem and self-worth have been realised a future direction needs to be set and aimed for. How do we aim for our dreams and desires? How do our children make their dreams come true? In the next chapter we will explore ways to set goals and make our dreams a reality.

7
SETTING GOALS AND REALISING YOUR DREAMS

Hold on tightly to your dreams and watch them grow as life's magic wand turns them into reality.

With our self-esteem and our self-worth intact we are now ready to aim for our goals and dreams. Everyone needs direction and it is up to each one of us to find our path and follow it. In this respect, children and teenagers are no different. As children grow up, they gain more and more control of their lives, and our role as parents is to guide and support them in whatever they choose to do. Too many teenagers leave school with no idea what they will do. We must get them to focus on small achievable goals when they are young. Then they can build up to larger goals as they grow older. This will help them acquire the skills needed to lead successful and fulfilling lives.

Goal setting and organisational skills will help your children plan their lives and accomplish their dreams. Our dreams and desires can be achieved if focus and direction are applied. Too many people drift from day to day, feeling they have achieved nothing, and children are no exception. In fact, children are very good at drifting along. Encouraging them to set goals gets them to put their thoughts into motion, taking responsibility and control of their own lives. But their goals must come from a real desire and passion to achieve, not from hurt, pain, fear, or just because they want to be better than someone else. Without desire and passion the drive to achieve will not be there.

Exercise for goal setting

1. Write down a list of all you want to achieve as a family; holidays, home, car and so on.
2. Write a 'what you all need to do' list to achieve each item on your list of desires.
3. Allow a realistic time for your family to achieve these things.
4. Make a separate list of your three most important family goals and put them on the fridge door or somewhere they will be seen every day.
5. Gather all the information you need to achieve your goals.
6. Stick up creative and inspiring posters about your goals.
7. Write an affirmation about achieving each goal.
8. Know that you will achieve your goals.
9. Share your goals with each other, and their progress.
10. Check the list of goals regularly and be flexible, changing it if and when it needs to be changed, but hold on to the dream and the desire to get there.

'How tos'

There is no time like the present to start helping your children map out their lives. Procrastination will not make their dreams and wishes come true. Find the time to sit down with your children and find out where they want to go and what they want to achieve. You cannot live their lives for them but you can help and support their dreams and goals. Some of their goals may seem too big and unobtainable but the idea is for your children to persist—keep them heading towards their dreams.

Children have to learn to be flexible as some things may stand in the way of their dreams. Your first priority is to work out what their wishes are no matter how big or small. Then put a time frame on them. Encourage your children to have daily, weekly, monthly, yearly and five-yearly goals. Once they have established their goals, get them to be specific about what they ask for. Their journal is a good place to write down their goals where they can look at them every day to stay focused on their desired outcome. The next thing is to encourage your children to see and feel what it is that they wish to achieve. They may like to get pictures or information on their goals and put them on their walls so they can see them every day. Encourage them to talk about their dreams and goals—a dream shared is a powerful experience and everyone likes to help make a dream come true. Perhaps your children can get in touch with someone they look up to who has achieved what they desire. Let your children know that mixing with other successful, positive children and adults is an advantage. Negative influences can be detrimental and may come in the form of friends who are not doing well or have no perceived future view. Keep your children motivated, building strong wills to succeed.

When your children have achieved their goals get them to tick the item off the list in their journal. Being able to look back in their books to see all the ticks and success they have achieved will spur them on to bigger and better things. Planning and goal setting are essential to leading organised dream-fulfilled lives.

Andrew, a young man I know, wrote to Qantas Airways when he was eight or nine years old. He had always wanted to be a pilot. They wrote him a lovely letter back explaining what he needed to do. Andrew wrote to them again when he was fifteen. Then he got in touch with universities to find out about available courses and spoke to some qualified pilots. He even went in search of a job near the local airport. He is living his desire. He worked at his grades, had posters all over his room, and put the letters from the airline in a place he could always see. He has direction and purpose.

Organised and prepared for life

Wouldn't it be nice to have an organised household, children who are perfect and know exactly what is going on, when and what they need to have at what time, never forgetting anything? Perhaps there are such households somewhere, but if your house is like mine we are doing our human best to be organised and prepared for life and we're not perfect. If it's not the school hat, it's the lunch that's been left behind, or perhaps it's an atlas left in the school desk . . . One day I raced off down the road to hear one child shouting they had no knickers on! Whatever it is I know that as a mother I have worn a rut in the road where my car travels up and down to the school.

My eldest is an extremely well-organised teenager, but as a little fellow he would forget all sorts of things. As a dutiful mother I would drop all the children off at school only to come home and find his sports bag, his lunch, or something he needed that particular day still sitting in the kitchen. I would race back down to the school clutching the item. Then one day his schoolmaster called me to one side. 'Mrs Lane-Smith,' he said. 'I've noticed how often you bring in things that your son has left behind. As from tomorrow if he leaves something behind—he leaves it behind. I don't want to see you until three o'clock!'

I was wounded. My poor boy, I thought, what will he do?

Will he burst into tears and have a horrible day? How could I do this to him?

He forgot a few things over the next week and it broke my heart to think he might be missing out on an activity or starving to death in the playground as everyone else gulped down their mothers' lovely homemade sandwiches at lunchtime. It was only a short time before he had organised himself. He knew what he had to do and we have never looked back.

Children need to be organised to build healthy minds, bodies and environments. If they are tidy in their mind they are tidy in their work and play. Being ready and organised in all they do builds their confidence and shows through in their attitude towards life in general. You can build up their organisational skills by making them responsible for getting their school clothes and extra-curricular items ready; keeping their rooms tidy; organising their own schedules and being on time. Speaking from personal experience it does take time. Sometimes I think we are all organised only to discover that, even though it left home, the PE bag is still in the boot of the car, or one child's lunch is in another child's bag. It may help to put a notice up on the fridge or kitchen door outlining what everyone must do on a particular day, with the time, equipment and clothes listed. Get them to read the list every day until they have learnt the routine. Encouraging them to use a timetable or diary can also have tremendous benefits for children, and parents.

I am a winner

Positive sayings to help your children reach their full potential

- I am confident in all I do—I am a winner.
- I make all the right decisions for myself when I need to put my life on the right path.
- My life has purpose, direction and meaning, now and always.

- I attract all the right people into my life to help me achieve my goals, dreams and wishes.
- I am good at everything I do.

The blossom tree

A meditation to make your children more confident and help them achieve anything they set out to do

Lie down and get really comfortable. There is nothing in this world to be afraid of. You have within you the ability to achieve anything you want to. Nothing can stop you.

Lay your arms and hands down by your side and close your eyes. I want you to feel yourself breathing in and out. With each breath in you feel love filling your whole body. With each breath out, I want you to imagine you are letting go of anything that has been bad or has upset you today. Just let it flow out of your body and away from you. Breathe in lots of love and breathe out, letting go of all the things you wish would go away. Let them float away on the breeze. As you breathe in and out, feel your body getting heavier and heavier; you are more and more relaxed. Now picture a big golden sun above your head sending down beautiful warm golden rays onto the top of your head. Feel the warmth and energy this sun is giving you. Feel the warmth and the golden rays flow down through your head to your shoulders and notice how you feel as this golden light now flows quickly and freely down through your arms, right down to the end of your fingertips. As the golden rays of sunshine pass through your body, feel how your body lights up like a sparkler with the golden rays of pure energy. Take these rays down your legs, right the way down to the very tips of your toes. See how your body sparkles and glows. Rays and rays of golden energy are bursting through you from the top of your head down to the tips of your toes. You are like a huge ball of golden sunshine.

Now imagine yourself as the tiny seed of a big tree in the ground. As you lie here you feel very safe, all curled up in the arms of the soil that surrounds you. Imagine your seed growing roots which spread out in the ground. Feel your roots dig deep into the soil. Imagine them reaching out far and wide into the earth. Ask your roots to suck up enough of the earth's water, vitamins and goodness for you to grow up healthy and strong towards the sky. As the goodness fills your body you see a shoot sprout from your seed through the earth's crust up into the fresh air. Feel the air, feel the wind, feel the sun's warm rays on your green shoots. You are growing bigger and bigger, stronger and stronger, as you grow into a magnificent tree. Your big brown trunk is straight, strong and sturdy. It sends out branches in all directions, reaching high into the sky, and far across the fields. A rain shower sprinkles your fresh leaves with pure clean water. It washes away all your fears and worries. Suddenly the sun comes out and dries the droplets of water and you feel positive and bright.

Flower buds open and your branches are covered with colourful petals. The smell of the flowers invites birds to swoop down and land on your branches. The birds sing and dance, happy to be with you. Butterflies flutter by, while bees hum and buzz. Red, yellow, orange, green, blue and purple flowers grow up around your trunk. Tiny elves and fairies dance and play around the flowers, sprinkling magic dust all over you. The magic dust gives you strength and courage to face any rough weather that might come your way. The ground beneath you supports you and keeps you balanced and straight. The earth feeds you energy from the soil, while the sun, wind and rain play and have fun with your branches and leaves. Other trees sprout up around you. They want to share their lives with you. Animals dart in and out of the trees. Perhaps you might like to talk to one of them?

When you have finished talking to your animal, you may open your eyes. Remember that you are loved and cared for. You are successful in everything you set out to do. You are clever, special and unique. You are a child of the universe. Thank yourself for being who you are.

The tree of life

A meditation to bring your child inner peace, a pure acceptance of themselves and others, a strength that is theirs to keep, and love and purpose into their life

Lie down, get really comfortable and close your eyes. As you lie here quiet and peaceful think about your breathing. Notice the rhythm of your breath. Feel the gift of love and life being given to you. As you breathe in, imagine an exquisite pure white light filling each and every part of your body. As you breathe out let go of anything that has upset you in any way. Let go of any bad thoughts and feelings and let them flow away as you breathe out. Forget what has happened in the past; we are here, now, in this moment. Breathe in . . . Breathe out . . .

Continue the gentle rhythm of your breath. Imagine yourself as the tiny seed of a tree, buried deep in the rich brown soil of Mother Earth. Look at the type of seed you are. Now think about the type of tree you want to become. With your tree in mind, imagine yourself growing roots that dig deep into the earth. See them going far and wide. Feel them holding the soil. Now see your roots sucking up enough food, water, goodness, vitamins and energy for your seed to become healthy and whole.

Suddenly, your seed is so full it explodes, sending your young green shoots into the fresh air. The wind and sunshine touch your skin. Feel its freshness. Feel how alive it is. Soak up its pure radiant energy.

As you grow, keep the picture of the kind of tree you want to be in your mind. See your trunk become strong, sturdy, straight. See your branches reach out in all directions. As the wind blows through your branches imagine it blowing away all fears, doubts, lies and dishonesty. As the rain falls upon you, feel it wash away any old negative feelings and emotions. And as the sun dries your leaves and branches, feel the positive vibrant thoughts and feelings expanding in you. As you stand here for all the world to see, know that you have direction and purpose; you have new life and new ideas as new sprouts appear and buds unfurl.

Know that even if the seasons or the weather change, you can take part and succeed in all life has to offer. You will always be able to adapt and be steadfast, whatever happens. When people see you, they will see a special unique part of nature that has its own role to play. They will see you standing with your own two feet on the ground and your head held high.

Remember that the earth will keep you balanced and stable. The sun and rain will feed you. The wind will rustle your leaves, but only when you are ready will you allow your leaves to fall, as in the autumn. Your branches are flexible and will not break as the wind howls. Life fills your veins. New rings of life are being formed continually within you. As the sun rises each day you have a new beginning—a fresh start.

Your tree is magnificent and beautiful. No one can take that away from you. Your roots are strong and deep, helping you make your unique mark in this world. Whatever tree you are—wave your arms, rustle your leaves. Share all of nature's beautiful gifts.

When you choose to open your eyes, know that your life is balanced and in harmony. It is a life filled with love, strength, courage and confidence. You are unique—let your light be seen.

Suggested Australian Bush Flower Essences

To build courage, faith and tenacity: Waratah
To gain and maintain focus: Turkey Bush

Parents' page

What can you do to get your life in order? If you are organised and have goals your children will mirror your actions. If you show them you have purpose they will want it too. So take the time to establish what you want out of life—set yourself goals and achieve them. You have a purpose. It is up to you to achieve your life's mission.

Look at every area of your life in detail and work out where you want to go, what you want to achieve, with whom and by when. Share your dreams and successes with your family. Organise your time. As parents we tend to devote so much time to our children, our spouses, the house and so on, that we tend to forget about ourselves and before we know it the days have turned into weeks and years have slipped by. Having an organised life and dreams to fulfil is magical.

Many people have a great deal of satisfaction using alternative therapies to help them achieve their dreams and goals. Kinergetics is fantastic for clearing any blockages that are stopping you from moving forward or achieving what you set out to do. Affirmations help many people because the written and spoken word are very powerful. Seeing dreams and goals in writing helps us to focus our thoughts and move in the direction of our desired goal. Australian Bush Flower Essences are also very powerful in the pursuit of goals. Taking a few drops every day will help you focus your thoughts and give you the courage to follow your dreams even when the going gets tough.

Focus on your dreams—positive sayings for direction and purpose in your life

- I know what I want to do, by when and with whom. My dreams are coming true for me now.
- I am focused in everything that I do. My life is in order and everything I do comes easily to me.

- I am a happy, confident and successful person in all I do.
- My life is on track for my family's highest purpose.

The wishing well—a meditation to help you acknowledge some of your dreams and goals

Lie or sit down and get really comfortable. Close your eyes. As you sit or lie here quiet and still take three long deep breaths. As you breathe in, feel the air filling you. As you breathe out, let go of any negative thoughts or fears you may have. Just relax. Continue to be aware of your breath and breathe slowly and calmly. Now imagine a beautiful white light streaming down from the heavens above. The white light totally engulfs you, both inside and out. Feel the light embrace you, filling you.

Imagine you are standing by a wishing well. Beside the wishing well is a bucket. Pick up the bucket and begin to fill it up with all your dreams and wishes. Be specific about your dreams and wishes, see them in detail, picture them in your mind as you put them in the bucket. It doesn't matter how big they are or how bizarre they may seem, put them in the bucket where all of them fit easily. When you have done this, grab hold of the rope attached to the bucket and use it to swing the bucket back into the wishing well. Release the rope gradually and watch the bucket travel down into the depths of the well—let go of the rope and with it, release all your hopes, dreams and wishes—bless them. When you hear the bucket hit the water all your hopes, dreams and wishes will be one with nature and the universe. They are becoming reality.

Now you know you can come back to the wishing well at any time if you want to change any of your hopes, dreams or goals. Just pick up the bucket and fill it again. A voice is listening to you and you are being given all the love and support you need to succeed on your journey—the journey of life.

Suggested Australian Bush Flower Essences

To build courage, a strong faith and tenacity: Waratah
To gain and maintain focus: Turkey Bush

We all have dreams and goals we would like to achieve but many of us put them in the too hard basket. Why? Because we lack conviction and motivation. If we truly want something our passion and desire will help us achieve it. In the next chapter we will look at how to get motivated and stay motivated.

8
MOTIVATION

Aim for the stars and catch every breath of wind to help you get there.

Revving your engine

Now that you have some idea about where you are heading as an individual or a family, you need to find the motivation to turn your thoughts and ideas into action and make them real.

How many times have you seen what needs to be done, but, instead, you do everything else except the thing you really need to do? Sometimes it is easier to remain preoccupied with everything else rather than sitting down to find out what it is you need, because fear of success or failure can sabotage your ability to take action.

Having been in the motivation game for many years, it is amazing to hear what people do to avoid what they really want from life. Being self-motivated requires a lot of work and self-discipline. Without motivation life seems to slip away from us but when motivated we seem able to do anything.

Self-motivation means putting your life into action with meaning and purpose. It is important your family is motivated to help each individual achieve their life's purpose. It means living each minute to the fullest and enjoying what you are doing. Self-motivation also means dealing with the fear of failure, being wrong, making mistakes. Being self-motivated can mean subjecting ourselves to difficult truths and experiencing some pain but it also leads to triumph and happiness. Children who experience fear of failure tend to go into their own world becoming reclusive and too frightened to try anything new in case it makes them look stupid or foolish.

If your children don't try they'll never know

Our lives and those of our children are being lived at an incredible pace. We seem to be living faster and faster and there never seem to be enough hours in the day to do all the things we want. Having some quiet time for ourselves seems a luxury.

For children to be successful they need to focus their energy in a positive way. They need to focus and channel their thoughts, feelings and imagination into a higher level of performance, while developing a positive outlook on life, encouraging challenges, looking out for opportunities and synchronicities placed before them every day, and keeping motivated enough to do what is needed for their highest purpose. They should be encouraged to try what life has to offer without fear of failure.

When things go wrong in our lives we tend to blame everything and everyone else, but we need to teach our children how to create positive outcomes in their lives by taking responsibility for their actions, reactions and interactions. Children have to learn that the process of growing and expanding can mean making mistakes. Taking away your children's limitations and boundaries can be scary for them especially when they have to do things for the first time. The fear of not doing something right or being made to look stupid can stop a child from attempting something that could change his or her life forever. Children need to be encouraged to give things a chance, whether it is a new type of food, a new relationship or an activity. They must understand that if they don't give something new a chance they will never be able to form an accurate opinion about it or know if they can do it and be successful at it. Help your children to understand that if they try something and they like it, it can enhance their senses.

Commitment

As parents we tend to project many of our own fears onto our children. In this way painful events in our lives can alter the way our children approach life too. If we are not prepared to give life a chance then why should our children? They look to us for example. Children absorb large amounts of information all the time. They need to be exposed to as much positive information and activity as possible so that they can make the best unbiased decisions.

Children need to acknowledge some sort of commitment. If they are allowed to flit from one thing to another without commitment they will have trouble committing to many important facets of life as they grow older. It requires some fine judgement on your part when asking your children to follow through with a commitment because if your children are miserable and hate what they are doing, they will block their own learning, making the whole exercise futile. Use your judgement, but be sensitive to their feelings, and allow a realistic time for them to follow through with commitment that will encourage the fulfilment of a task.

Encouragement, love and support

As we all know, trying something out for the first time can be nerve-racking and scary, making us bite our nails, find other things to do, or run for cover—encouragement and support are vital. When children know there is someone who can pick them up, dust them off and put them back on track they are usually willing to have a go.

I have always had a fear of speaking in public, but I had no qualms about sending my son out to be seen and heard in public. I encouraged him to join a choir, take part in plays, debating teams and so on, and I have always been there to love and support him in any of these activities, especially when he was playing an extra-special part. There is one instance that stands out in my mind. I had encouraged my son to take part in a special presentation that would have unnerved anyone, but with encouragement, love and support my son performed solo for the first time.

I had taken my family with me to the United States for a professional speakers' conference. I had never seen so many speakers in one place—there were over 2000 delegates at the conference. I attended four days of lectures and my son attended the children's conference, which had lectures on public speaking, self-esteem, image, goal setting and much more. At the end of the four days, four out of the ninety children were picked to give a talk to the adult delegates. My son was one of them.

As we walked towards the room where my son was to speak, my heart was pounding and my palms were sweaty—I was nervous and wondered whether I was going to make it to the end of his speech. I had butterflies in my stomach when he was introduced to an audience of over one thousand delegates. My eyes filled with tears and my pride overflowed as I listened to this smartly dressed young man, all of ten years old, deliver his five-minute speech without a hitch. The audience gave him a standing ovation. It was even more moving that he did not stutter once, a problem that had been occurring more and more in his everyday language. Perhaps I had carried all his fears on my back, but I am always there to support my children and I like to think they are there for me too.

My experience proved to me that, with encouragement, motivation and a dream in sight, children can achieve great results that build their self-esteem, confidence and self-worth. My son was motivated and focused on what he had to do. Having never done anything like this before in his life, his drive helped him to overcome his fear and the result was success.

Mistakes are lessons in disguise

We all make mistakes—they are life's lessons. We must not allow our mistakes to degrade us or make us feel stupid; they happen to help us change what we are doing. When we have made a mistake we often worry about what other people will think of us and what they might say about us to others; we feel guilt and shame and then proceed to put ourselves down. Children feel this way too. They assess what has happened and then label themselves as no good, failures, idiots, or useless, instead of holding their heads high, feeling proud of what they have been able to achieve, and then trying again and again until they succeed.

Try, try, again

If children wish to succeed teach them to try again. If something is proving too hard for them, help them find a way to succeed and with persistence they will finally win through.

How many people do we see doing extremely well for themselves—the high achievers? And why do so many people seem to enjoy putting them down? When these people fall they seem to fall hard, but they don't just lie there, they get up and start again. They are the real self-starters. Self-motivated people have the drive to succeed and achieve what they want from life.

Janet

Recently, when I was discussing future prospects with Janet, a very dear friend of mine, we got talking about the past and how we got where we are now. Janet told me she felt she had won and lost her greatest dream. She is a very focused person and has made many of her dreams and goals come true but one day circumstances changed the course of her life. Her greatest dream was to own a magnificent home with beautiful views over the sea. She had made that dream a reality, until one day, like many other people whose lives are disrupted by stock market crashes or some sudden financial crisis, she faced losing her beautiful home along with many other investments. When the day came for her to move out of her dream home she sat in her empty bedroom and cried her heart out. 'What have I done to deserve this?' she anguished. 'Why must I lose my biggest dream and accomplishment?'

With time and perseverance Janet now has her life back on track. She has rebuilt her business and is saving every penny in order to buy her own home again. Her life is busy but she has a goal in sight. She is motivated and determined to make her dream come true once more. Janet was lucky, she had many friends to help her through her time of need. She always says how grateful she is to have had the love and support of her friends and family who have kept her focused and motivated, helping her rebuild her life.

The secret of success is knowing who we are, and where we want to go. It is important to follow our own dreams and goals and not those of other people. Being self-motivated means putting our dreams into action.

Lack of self-motivation—signs to look for

- apathy
- spending too much time alone and not joining in activities

- changes in eating habits
- tiredness or insomnia
- sudden change in behaviour or attitude
- lack of self-esteem
- depression

A checklist of things your children can do to become self-motivated

1. Write down a list of your priorities.
2. Put a plan in place to achieve your goals and remain flexible if changes need to be made.
3. Build your self-esteem.
4. Mix with other self-motivated people.
5. Leave behind the people that bring you down.
6. Control any stressful situations so that you feel safe rather than fearful.
7. Read motivational books and attend motivational groups.
8. Talk with your school counsellor or see a therapist to help you through the difficult times.
9. Learn from your mistakes and let them go.

Motivated for action

Positive sayings to help create motivation and commitment in your children

- I am confident and successful in all I say and do.
- I have all the people I need in my life to help me be the best person I can.
- I am a positive happy person.
- I am committed and dedicated to making my dreams come true.

Ride the pathway to your dreams

A meditation to guide your children along the path to their dreams and goals

Either sit down with your back straight or lie down. Get really comfortable. Gently close your eyes. Now take three deep breaths nice and slowly, breathing in all the way down, filling your lungs with air, and breathing out, letting go of any fears or worries.

Imagine a beautiful light streaming down from the sky touching your head. Feel the warmth of this light as it travels through your head, down your neck, all the way to your arms and through your body, down your legs to your toes. Feel your body glow with warmth and light. As you sit or lie here the light changes into all the colours of the rainbow.

Just in front of you is a bicycle. Have a good look at it. What does it look like? Has it got big or little wheels? Imagine yourself climbing onto the bike and feel your feet touch the pedals. As you start to pedal the bike you may find it hard, so imagine yourself cycling along with determination and purpose as if you know exactly where you are going. Look at the ground underneath your bike. Is it rocky or smooth? As you pedal it is getting easier and easier and you find yourself going really fast. The wind is in your face, sweeping back your hair. You feel the air clearing all your worries and fears away. You feel a growing desire to get to your destination. Point your bike towards your destination and feel how you fly along. Put power and energy into your pedalling. As you are cycling along, ask yourself what is it you need to help you along your path. Take time to ask the question and listen for the answer.

Now you know you are being guided along the right path. If at any time you feel you want to change direction or you need help, ask and listen for the answer. When you are on the right path you will pedal your bicycle with ease. If it becomes hard to ride your bicycle, ask if there is an easier way for you to reach your destination. Now I'm going to leave you here pedalling with ease and when you are ready you can stop your bicycle and get off wherever you feel comfortable.

Suggested Australian Bush Flower Essences

To release anxiety: Dog Rose, Crowea
To gain inner balance: Jacaranda, Bush Fuchsia
To relieve depression: Kapok Bush, Flannel Flower, Wild Potato Bush, Red Grevillea
To release and let go of frustration: Old Man Banksia, Black-eyed Susan, Jacaranda, Sunshine Wattle, Red Grevillea

Parents' page

If your children suffer from lack of motivation it can be exhausting for you, and if you are not careful their lack of motivation can rub off on you. It is important to lead your children by example. Talk and listen to your children about their aims and goals and be supportive in whatever they do. Give them encouragement and even offer them incentives.

The people they choose as friends are very important. Although you cannot change their friends for them you can help them make better choices of their own.

Ask them to plan ahead and if they feel that planning for the whole week is too much, get them to plan daily or even hourly. Keeping a diary is a great asset and stands them in good stead later in life.

How do you cope with unmotivated children without bringing yourself and the whole family down?

- Remain positive and motivated yourself.
- Take time for yourself, for instance go for a walk or play your favourite sport.
- Set your life as an example for your children to follow.

Attend classes or read motivational books and leave them around the house for your children to see.

- Learn to meditate daily and take time to relax.
- Try not to lose your cool. If you lose your temper then everyone becomes more frustrated and relationships break down.

Motivation needs to be ongoing in all we do. Encourage your children to keep a journal to record all their dreams and goals. Share meditations with them to help them enhance their thoughts and dreams. Help them to relax by using aromatherapy and massage techniques to put them in a frame of mind that is calm and clear. When your motivation wanes have a session with your Kinergetics therapist to find out what is blocking your pathway to success. Most importantly of all focus on your dreams and goals at all times and make a commitment to achieve them.

Success—positive sayings to help you keep motivated and focused

- I am calm, relaxed and motivated at all times.
- I am supported and am being supportive to myself and those around me.
- I face life's challenges in a positive successful way and am highly successful in all I do and say.

The tunnel of dreams—a meditation to help set your life in the right direction

Take three long deep slow breaths. As you do this close your eyes and feel yourself sink further and further down. Imagine yourself floating in a calm, quiet and still space. Now imagine rays of light pouring down through your body, all the way down from the top of your head to the tips of your toes. Still floating in your calm, quiet space you go deeper and deeper into this space. As you float you are drawn along, and know you are moving in this direction for a specific reason. You feel the strength of your body and soul being enhanced as you travel down a tunnel filled with all your hopes, dreams and aspirations. Reach out and take them as you travel along. Take your time travelling down the tunnel. You are not in a hurry, relax and enjoy the floating sensation.

At the end of the tunnel you see a light. When you arrive at the light you have the confidence, motivation and clarity to achieve everything you wish for. If at any time you would like to ask for help or guidance, ask in the beauty and serenity of this place and listen for the reply.

Now you are going in the right direction. As you come out into the light you look around and see you have all the people needed to help you achieve everything you want. As you gently bring yourself back to the here and now be aware of your feelings and thoughts. Let only positive thoughts fill your being now and always.

Suggested Australian Bush Flower Essences

To release anxiety: Dog Rose, Crowea
To gain inner balance: Jacaranda, Bush Fuchsia
To relieve depression: Kapok Bush, Flannel Flower, Wild Potato Bush, Red Grevillea
To relieve fatigue: Macrocarpa, Sunshine Wattle, Old Man Banksia
To release and let go of frustration: Old Man Banksia, Black-eyed Susan, Jacaranda, Sunshine Wattle, Red Grevillea

It all sounds pretty simple, setting goals and motivating ourselves to act, but the road to many dreams may not be easy. We live in a stressful world. We have so many things to do and so many dreams to be fulfilled in what seems a very short time. In the next chapter we will find ways for you and your children to deal with stress.

9
OVERCOMING STRESS AT HOME

Our path in life may not always be smooth and even, but we can choose how we put our feet on the ground.

We are now on the pathway to our dreams. We have established where we plan to go, how we are going to get there and that we are going to do anything to succeed. But not everything will go exactly as planned. We all have highs and lows and as we go along our life's path we will encounter many challenges and obstacles, and these may be stressful.

Stress is the fear of the known and the unknown. We feel it most when we are taken out of our comfort zone. A little stress is healthy, it gives us our drive and enhances our performance. When our stress level is too high, we experience internal or external conflict which affects our mental, physical and spiritual well-being. Everyone experiences stress but how they behave in different situations depends on the individual, their environment and their emotional and mental makeup.

If one person within the family is stressed then everyone is stressed and this can cause disagreements, fights, arguments and tension. It may mean the family don't spend time together.

Some people choose to escape stress through drugs and alcohol. Some just withdraw from the situation so they don't have to face their problems. If everything becomes too much it can lead to a total breakdown of the family.

Often it is our expectations that cause conflict and the level of stress that results can depend on the situation. Some of the highest stressors in life are the death of a family member, divorce and separation. Conversely we become stressed when we are bored with life, or our needs and desires are not being met. We can also feel stressed doing the same thing over and over again because we are not moving further along our life's path. If we find ourselves in the same old rut day after day we may either not see or not receive the opportunities life has to offer.

There are many different theories about how stress is experienced, but many believe that stress is experienced three ways: internally or externally, acutely or chronically, and a combination of both. Acute stress usually comes from a situation that is immediate, short term and painful. A classic example of acute stress is having to stand up and give a speech—the palms of your hands become clammy, your hands shake, your throat feels tight and your voice is croaky. All of these signs go away once the stressful situation is over.

Chronic stress is experienced over a longer period of time and may recur. It is caused by our perception of what is happening around us. After constant stress the body becomes so traumatised that sometimes it never fully recovers and relapses may occur. A combination of both acute and chronic stress can be experienced especially when there has been a history of abuse, whether physical or emotional. Initially the stress may be acute but because it happens over and over again it becomes chronic.

We experience internal stress when our physical and emotional needs are not being met. Children's needs are fairly basic, such as food, shelter and security, but if these are not being met children become frightened and stressed. Children react the same way as the people around them. Quite often this is the result of poor communication or a misunderstanding. When we suppress or repress our feelings and emotions we are not being true to ourselves. Unexpressed emotions cause anxiety and fear, especially if the stressful situation happens again and again. Internal stress is also experienced when our self-esteem has taken a battering and we feel sorry for ourselves, telling ourselves we are stupid instead of being able to move on. Children are particularly adept at putting themselves down.

We experience external stress when pressures or frustrations come from situations and people around us. It may be that the situation we are in is not comfortable because it is foreign to us. It may be that someone is expecting something from us and either we don't know how to react to that expectation, or perhaps it actually conflicts with our own expectations, values and beliefs.

Another time when external stress may be experienced is when we don't have enough time to complete everything we want to achieve and we overload our lives. A classic example is when our children are asked to complete a school project by a certain date. Many families are already overloaded with extra-curricular activities. Perhaps all that needs to be done is to go to the library for information books, but you never seem to have the time to stop and get them. Every time you drive past the library the kids call for you to stop, but as usual time is precious and you must be somewhere else. You keep trying to make time while the kids get more and more frustrated. As the due date for the project looms there is a mad rush to get cardboard, research the information and borrow library books. The project is done in a hurry and although it gets finished it may not be done as well as it could have been. Children are no different from us—they experience stress too.

Children's stress factors

Information overload

Computers, mobile phones, television, radio and the Internet provide our children with information they have to retain and assimilate. Everything is moving so fast in the information age that information overload is a reality—especially for children.

Competition

I am a great believer in healthy competition but in today's society many children wonder if they will have a job at the end of their schooling. If parents don't enrol their children into extra-curricular activities they fear their children will be left behind. Children who don't engage in these activities often feel left out. Other children may ridicule them saying their parents don't care for them, or can't afford to look after them. Sometimes they are taunted with being stupid. So whether or not you enrol your children in competitive classes they will face stress from their peers.

Death of a close family member, friend or pet

The death of a loved one is one of the highest stressors children will experience. When their pet dies or has an accident, children experience grief and anguish, a sense of loss and emptiness, which causes a lot of stress. Many children become quiet and cry frequently, some may repress their feelings trying to be brave. Others become loud and aggressive, to show they don't care that much and life must go on. No matter how they respond to death, such a tragic situation brings many tears and much heartache, and often sickness or periods of fatigue.

Blended families

The joining together of children through a new relationship or marriage can cause huge amounts of stress if the children do not get on together, or if their core values are different. Some children may experience different emotions—for example, jealousy or anger—and not know how to express their feelings in order to live together harmoniously. Such changes to the family structure can cause stress until everyone has adjusted to the new way of living. Children of blended families may feel they have to forget the previous partner or call the new partner mum or dad, which may cause resentment and unacceptable behaviour. This in turn may cause stress in the relationship between partners and children.

Arrival of a new family member, for example a new baby

Many children feel a sense of jealousy when a new baby comes home. They may feel left out and think their parents are spending too much time with the newcomer. Children may use outrageous behaviour to draw attention back to themselves. Some children attack the newcomer or pretend that the baby has done something wrong to make them seem naughty. This causes major stress for the parents who are trying to build their family. They have to find ways to resolve the situation, which can be tiring and stressful.

Role changes

Today many men work at home while women go out to work and have busy careers. Some parents are confused about their appropriate role in the relationship and our children pick up this confusion. Such confusion causes anxiety about what is expected in each person's role to perform successfully in the family.

Many men have been brought up to believe they are the head of the family, the main provider. When the role of provider is shared or given to the female, some males lose their self-worth and self-esteem, causing arguments, resentment, anger and fear.

Our society has been brought up to believe that housework and child rearing are women's work, but times have changed. Some men prefer to stay home and do these chores, while others cannot get work outside the home but their wives can. As long as both partners accept the change in roles and consider either role as an invaluable asset the relationship can succeed.

Some men may become worried or jealous that their wives are more successful than them, and this can cause tension in the home. Children need to learn that everyone has a role to play regardless of gender, age or race. The goal is to play their part as well as they can and be prepared to adapt when circumstances change.

Sickness or perceived sickness

Often when children see something frightening on television, such as a person with a bad stomach ache that turns out to be life-threatening, they imagine they have a stomach ache too. They become afraid they've got what the person on television had and become fearful.

Children who have an illness, whether it is as serious as leukaemia or glandular fever, or as common as flu, need to learn how to cope and find ways to keep motivated and positive.

Marriage breakdown

Your children go through divorce too. Whether you are a grownup or a little person, you know what is going on and can feel the emotions and disruptions within your lives.

Low self-esteem

If we don't feel good about who we are, we worry about what other people think. Children can be very cruel to one another. They can be painfully blunt and more truthful than adults.

Signs of stress

Sandra

Sandra, aged 11, was experiencing problems at home. When her father was home her parents argued constantly. When he was away Sandra was more relaxed. Then the day came when dad decided to tell the family he was moving out permanently. Everything was in turmoil.

During the separation Sandra continued with her studies as best she could but a week before the court case for the divorce Sandra became violently ill, rolling around clutching her stomach. She had headaches, vomited, was dizzy, anxious and nervy. Her mother was extremely worried and took her to see their doctor who had tests done, but there was nothing wrong with Sandra.

Sandra stayed off school for the next week until the day after the court case. When she found out she was allowed to live with her mother her stomach pains disappeared. She had been worried that she might have to live with her father and would be left alone while he travelled for his work. He was always busy and never there to help when Sandra needed him. She had become so stressed it had made her ill.

Here are some signs to look for when children and teenagers are stressed (a classic example is when they have to get up in front of their class and give a speech):

- sweating
- shaking

- shortness of breath
- poor eating habits, for instance, over- or under-eating
- nausea
- dizziness
- headaches
- aching muscles
- anxiousness
- fearfulness
- mood swings
- poor decision-making
- poor concentration.

Studies have shown if stress is not dealt with properly, children may suffer from physical health problems, for instance asthma, back problems, ulcers and so on.

Responding to stress

We have the choice to run away from the conflicts that cause stress and pretend they aren't happening, put up with them until next time, or face our problems and deal with them head on. This can be scary for children and teenagers too, but the sooner we teach our children to take responsibility the quicker they will develop. Emotions need to be released, not repressed; suppressing emotions only causes more stress.

How your children and teenagers can deal with stress

Teach your children to manage or change the external stress factors—the things affecting them on the outside. If they feel their lives are dull and boring ask them to look at what they are doing and change it so that life is not one long boring routine. Some children don't even like to walk the same way home from school every day—help them to change their outlook.

Sometimes they may have to change their lifestyle, especially when there have been changes within the family such as a financial downturn, marriage breakdown, house move, change of schools, and other changes to their routine. Moving from place to place can be very stressful especially when it involves making new friends.

Your children can learn and practise self-development techniques to help them grow mentally, physically and spiritually. Children grow faster when they interact with other children, and self-development groups are excellent for building children's self-esteem and confidence.

They can also learn relationship strategies where interpersonal relationships can be explored. Our relationships today are very complex. Communication and listening are the keys to all relationships. Without communication stress builds up as confusion, animosity and mistrust replace openness and shared values. Sometimes what one person says and the other hears are two different things. Clear, effective, honest and open communication is crucial. Listening is a big part of communicating too, as we tend to hear only what we want to hear.

Exercise is great for stress relief. When children are cooped up they act like caged animals. They need physical exercise. Make sure that your children and teenagers have a sport or physical pursuit to help relieve their pent-up energies and frustrations.

Relaxation techniques such as meditation and yoga are beneficial too. Teach your children the importance of relaxation and calming the mind to release stress, and share your experiences with them.

Teaching them to look after their diet is important. We all eat too much or too little, or the wrong sorts of food, when we are stressed. In times of stress it is important to pay attention to our dietary needs. We have to be very careful with our intake of sugar and white flour as we look for quick energy boosts in stressful times and often use sugars instead of carbohydrates. Many of our children's mood swings are directly linked to what they eat. For example sugar can bring a quick high but this is also followed by a real low.

Be calm, relax

Positive sayings to help ease a busy lifestyle

- I let go of everything that is making me feel uneasy or unwell. I let go of all my worries now.
- I am calm and relaxed. When anything causes me stress I am able to deal with it confidently and well.
- Everything helps me to grow into a stronger person.
- I take responsibility for my life only and do not take on other people's problems as my own.

The genie in the cave

A meditation to help your children relax and become whole again, keeping them in touch with their inner self

Lie down and get really comfortable. Gently close your eyes. Imagine a beautiful golden light streaming down onto your head. This beautiful golden light spreads down your neck and across your shoulders. It flows quickly, and gently, down your right arm, all the way down to the end of each and every one of your precious little fingers. You see the light spread down your left arm, all the way down to your other precious fingers. The golden light flows stronger as it goes all the way through your body, down your right leg to your toes. You feel it growing stronger again as it flows down your left leg, all the way down to each of your toes.

The golden light moves around your body like energy, making you stronger and stronger each moment that passes. It fills every part of you.

As you lie here quiet and still, imagine you are sitting on a beach. In the background you can hear the waves rolling onto the shore. The sun is shining above you and the sand feels warm. The waves roll in and the sound relaxes you more and more.

You see dolphins leaping in and out of the water, playing a game with the waves. They laugh and chatter as they dive in and out of the sea. The dolphins see you sitting on the beach and come closer to shore. They ask you if you would like to go for a ride with them. Reach out and take hold of a dolphin's fin. Suddenly you speed through the water fast—so fast the water washes all your cares and worries away—feel them whisked away in the bright blue sea.

The dolphins dive suddenly and you go deeper and deeper in the water until you reach a beautiful underwater cave. The cave is filled with air and has a ledge for you to sit on, so climb up and sit down

All around you, the walls glimmer and shine with brightly coloured sparkles. Rainbows shine all around you where the water splashes up and hits the ledge. Beside you is a lamp. You pick up the lamp and rub it as Aladdin did in the wonderful fairytale. Suddenly a genie pops out. Ask the genie his name. The genie offers you three wishes to help you to become calm and relaxed, and be able to deal with any problems in your life. Make your three wishes.

'Done! Now you must trust that the best will happen,' the genie says, and he disappears back into the lamp.

When you are ready, the dolphins will take you back to the shore and you will sit on the sand once more. If you want to stay longer in the cave you may—it is a very safe place. If you want to ask the dolphins how to solve a particular problem, ask them and listen to what they say. Only you can make the things you wished for happen.

You can come back to the cave any time. The dolphins will be there when you need them. When you open your eyes you will be calm and relaxed and feel confident in all you do.

Suggested Australian Bush Flower Essences

To cope with accidents or trauma: Boronia, Jacaranda, Sundew, Red Lily, Mountain Devil, Fringed Violet
To release anxiety: Dog Rose, Crowea
To deal with appetite disorders: Bottle Brush, Sturt Desert Rose
To gain and maintain balance: Jacaranda, Bush Fuchsia, Crowea
To help control bed wetting: Red Helmet, Dog Rose
To give relief to breathing problems: Sunshine Wattle, Five Corners, Tall Yellow Top
For relieving constipation: Bluebell, Bottle Brush and Boronia
To release and let go of depression: Kapok Bush, Flannel Flower, Wild Potato Bush, Red Grevillea
To alleviate diarrhoea: Paw Paw
To combat fatigue: Macrocarpa, Sunshine Wattle, Old Man Banksia
To release and let go of frustration: Old Man Banksia, Black-eyed Susan, Jacaranda, Sunshine Wattle, Red Grevillea
For the relief of headaches: Emergency Essence, Five Corners, Paw Paw, Sturt Desert Rose
To relieve insomnia: Black-eyed Susan, Crowea, Boronia
To alleviate nausea: Dog Rose, Paw Paw
To reduce nervousness: Dog Rose, Black-eyed Susan, Jacaranda
To alleviate the after-effect of shock: Emergency Essence, Fringed Violet

Parents' page

A personal affirmation

I live my own life, changing my attitudes to suit my specific needs and desires. My personality is wonderful. I love who I am. I can only change my life not the lives of others. I am guiding my children and teenagers along their own paths.

Top family stressors

Here is a list of the top ten family stressors, some 50 per cent of which are connected with a lack of time-management.

1. Money.
2. Children's behaviour.
3. Not enough couple time.
4. An unequal share of household duties.
5. Trying to communicate with children.
6. Lack of time for oneself.
7. Guilt at not being able to do enough.
8. Interpersonal relationships.
9. Insufficient family time for play.
10. An over-committed family agenda.

How to cope if you are stressed

Depending on what type of person you are, you have your own special needs, desires and possible outcomes. Life is what you make of it. You can choose to change or stay as you are. If you choose to make changes be prepared for a new way of life. We must look deeply at our lives and work out our priorities. This is difficult for parents because our children and our spouses mean so much to us. If you notice you are stressed, step back a pace or two and breathe. Have you ever noticed that you forget to breathe when you are under stress?

You may feel you need to seek professional help with your problems. Never be ashamed of seeking therapy. Remember there is always someone who can help. Please refer to the resources section at the back of the book for a list of contacts. Here are a number of suggestions to help relieve your stress:

1. Seek relationship counselling or attend a relationship strategy course.

2. Seek sex counselling or attend a course to learn more about sexual partnerships.
3. Find out about and attend time-management or stress-management courses.
4. Find out what it is you are interested in for your own self-development—spiritual, mental or physical—and do it!
5. Do something you enjoy like reading, or take up a hobby.
6. Exercise frequently.
7. Set goals and revitalise your vision of the future.
8. Keep in touch with people around you and keep up-to-date with what is going on.
9. Nurture yourself; take a long soak in the bath and ask other family members to help with the household chores.
10. When you can afford to, engage a cleaner, gardener, or handy help to take the pressure off you so you can all enjoy quality family time together.

These are just a few ideas, I am sure you can think of many more. The idea is to let people know you are stressed and why. Then find solutions to alleviate the pressure. Remember, it is okay to ask for help.

All the alternative therapies mentioned in Part Two can help you deal with life's challenges and stress-related situations. Deal with situations and stressors immediately so they don't build up or get out of control. If the problems are recurring then some Kinergetics may be required to remove the blockages that prevent you from moving on. I like to have a massage and relax in a warm, lavender bath. I fill my bathroom with candles and soft relaxing music and my cares seem to evaporate in the peaceful atmosphere. Emergency Essence is a very effective stress-reliever in times of strife. Life seems to improve more quickly when you use positive sayings and prayers. I am always grateful when I see how life gets better with a little faith and conviction in my beliefs.

Right time, right place—positive sayings to give you clarity throughout your life's journey

- I am calm and relaxed in all situations and am able to see how to deal with each situation clearly.
- Everything happens to me for a reason. I am drawing everything I need to myself for my highest purpose.
- Everything that happens to me happens at the right time, and I have all the necessary resources to deal with any situation quickly and effectively.
- I take responsibility for my life only and do not take on other people's problems as my own.

Row, row, row your boat a meditation to help you in times of stress

In times of stress you may find that you need to meditate more frequently than usual to get the benefit of your meditations.

Take three long slow deep breaths. As you breathe in, imagine a beautiful white light filling you, and as you breathe out, imagine all your fears and worries leaving your body. See the white light fill your whole body. Lie and watch it gently flow within you. You feel safe and secure. You feel loved and cared for. Now, imagine the white light flows within you, and all around your body, completely sealing you in a cocoon. This cocoon of light protects you at all times, and especially in times of stress.

Imagine you are standing on a riverbank. Look around. See the beautiful colours of nature in the bushes and flowers growing on the bank. Smell the fresh air swirling around you. Butterflies flit from flower to flower. Fish leap in and out of the water. The sun warms you as it shines on you. The sky is a deep blue without a cloud in sight. You notice a little boat down near the water's edge. You climb into the boat and pick up the oars. You want to get to the other side of the river. Look at the bank opposite and see where all the people and things you want are. You start rowing across the water to the other side. As you row, the oars sweep deeply into the clear water. Your body relaxes as you let go of any tension within. Nature caresses and massages your body with love. Love fills your heart, mind, spirit and soul. All fears and worries are left in the wake of your boat. You are on track—on the right path for you. The water is calm but a gentle breeze comes up behind you, speeding you along, guiding you to the other side. You climb out of the boat. Then the people you need around you for your highest purpose surround you, greeting you with hugs and kisses. Acknowledge them and start walking up the track ahead of you. You notice the ground is smooth and you walk with ease.

As you walk along the track you leave behind any situations that have upset you and you trust you are heading in the right direction. If you are unsure which direction to take, ask the birds flying around you, heralding you. Listen to what they say. If you want, you can ask one of them to take you for a flight in the blue sky. You are as free as a bird. When you are ready open your eyes. You are relaxed and clear about what you are doing in your life. You can cope with stressful situations with ease and certainty.

Suggested Australian Bush Flower Essences

To cope with accidents or trauma: Boronia, Jacaranda, Sundew, Red Lily, Mountain Devil, Fringed Violet
To release anxiety: Dog Rose, Crowea
To deal with appetite disorders: Bottle Brush, Sturt Desert Rose
To gain and maintain balance: Jacaranda, Bush Fuchsia, Crowea
To help control bed wetting: Red Helmet, Dog Rose

To give relief to breathing problems: Sunshine Wattle, Five Corners, Tall Yellow Top

For relieving constipation: Bluebell, Bottle Brush and Boronia

To release and let go of depression: Kapok Bush, Flannel Flower, Wild Potato Bush, Red Grevillea

To alleviate diarrhoea: Paw Paw

To combat fatigue: Macrocarpa, Sunshine Wattle, Old Man Banksia

To release and let go of frustration: Old Man Banksia, Black-eyed Susan, Jacaranda, Sunshine Wattle, Red Grevillea

For the relief of headaches: Emergency Essence, Five Corners, Paw Paw, Sturt Desert Rose

To relieve insomnia: Black-eyed Susan, Crowea, Boronia

To alleviate nausea: Dog Rose, Paw Paw

To reduce nervousness: Dog Rose, Black-eyed Susan, Jacaranda

To alleviate the after-effect of shock: Emergency Essence, Fringed Violet

To control smoking: Boronia, Bottle Brush

We have covered many subjects designed to help individuals find direction, motivation, build healthy relationships and deal with life's challenges. Next we will learn how to express feelings and emotions that arise when we face life's challenges.

10
CREATIVE EXPRESSION

Teach your children to express themselves through the windows of their souls. Teach them to be honest and true to themselves and be open minded to absorb the wisdom they need to develop into successful, loving adults.

The ability to express our innermost feelings creatively is crucial in all our relationships, even our relationship with ourselves. Each one of us needs to be able to express ourselves and communicate our thoughts and feelings in our own way. We must know how to express ourselves vocally and in our body language to show the world who we are. When we are true to ourselves, we affirm ourselves to others and they know where they stand in our relationships with them. Sometimes this means we feel vulnerable, which can be nerve-racking, but if we use our intuition we can deal with our problems. If we are afraid of expressing ourselves we suppress our feelings and thoughts which isn't healthy.

We have been given emotions and feelings for a reason. Our feelings must be acknowledged. Even anger has a positive side. Expression of the self can be quite confronting for some, but with perseverance and trust in yourself and the universe miracles can happen.

If we suppress or bottle up our feelings and emotions they

build up and eventually tempers flare. Words blurted out in the heat of the moment express the things that enrage us as well as feelings we have stored away through suppression and fear. Our creative expression flows through us mentally, physically and spiritually and when any of these areas are blocked we experience pain, hurt and frustration. We need to release and let go of our emotions and feelings so we can move on in life. Otherwise our lives become stale and we stagnate. Our creative energy can be expressed through painting, craft, sport, or through our work. If we suppress this energy we become bored or we may find the task laborious and tedious. Aim to enjoy what you are doing and have a passion for life.

Our society encourages freedom of speech and it is good to see our schools teaching children to speak freely, voicing their opinions and thoughts through decision-making, problem solving and creative activities. Our children are learning to get in touch with their emotions and express them positively. Children are very imaginative and creative. They need to develop their creativity continually, otherwise they may have trouble achieving their goals.

To express ourselves successfully we must get in touch with ourselves and our real feelings, and convey them to others in a positive manner. If we express ourselves on the spur of the moment without thinking we may say things we don't really mean or convey a negative message. Teach your children to express their feelings in a positive manner, not only to others but to themselves. Positive self talk is a very good way to build healthy self-esteem.

Respect for one another

Children need to know they can speak honestly and openly, being true to themselves. They must remember to respect others' beliefs and values even if they don't share them. Teach your children to communicate successfully and not in a way that causes harm to themselves or others. You can teach them guidelines to express their feelings and emotions. For example, they should understand that anger and frustration are emotions to be dealt with and are part of life, but violence and physical abuse are never acceptable. Verbal or mental abuse is just as damaging as physical abuse, but the physical signs are less obvious. Respecting what others think and feel is important. Families need to discuss their feelings to air any suppressed emotions. We can't always be right or always be in control. Listening to another person's point of view expands our outlook on life. Sometimes we see a point of view we hadn't thought of, or realise we may have been blinkered, limited or selfish.

Control

When people feel out of control or over-controlled it stops them doing what their life requires of them. Nobody needs to be controlled or to control another. We must be aware of our personal power. This is particularly true of children who need to be guided, not controlled. Control causes fear and guilt which leads to abnormal behaviour. Control is very limiting.

Some people believe that expressing anger is inappropriate behaviour. Anger can make us feel as though we are out of control but there are times when being out of control helps us to experience the emotions and the problems we face. If we hide from our emotions, our problems may recur at a later date to try us again. Denied feelings turn into emotional pain, causing low self-esteem. In many cases addiction is the result of denied or repressed pain. Anger can be a positive, reactive emotion. How many vegetable gardens have been planted after an argument with a spouse? At the end of an argument we have so much energy to release.

Many things induce anger and as parents we accept that

our children will feel anger too. Here is a list of behaviour that can cause anger and pain:

- name calling
- shouting, yelling or raising the voice in a threatening manner
- criticism
- intimidation
- lying or deceitful behaviour
- cruelty or unkindness
- disapproval
- breaking promises
- laying blame or guilt
- violence or the threat of violence
- lack of love or attention
- manipulation and control.

Are you or your child regularly witness to this type of behaviour?

Signs to identify when children are hiding their anger

1. They become sarcastic or say things out of character.
2. They put off things they should be doing.
3. They spend more time in bed, or in their room alone.
4. They are agitated, tire easily and have difficulty going to sleep.
5. Their eating habits change and they may feel sick.
6. They are flippant, or unusually loud and happy, to keep the peace.
7. They lose their zest for life and get bored easily.
8. They seem depressed or sad.
9. They are late because they want attention.

A classic example of this last sign is when Will is getting ready for school in the morning. Everyone is busy. Mum and dad race around trying to make the school lunches, ironing shirts and making breakfast. Will's brothers and sisters have their own things to get ready. Who is there to help Will? Many children like Will find this an excellent time to go slow just to get attention. They get in the shower and afterwards, instead of getting dressed properly, they sit in their room for half an hour 'off with the fairies'. Will wants something done and he isn't getting any help so he's moving slowly. What happens next is a daily event in many households each morning. Tempers flare and everyone gets stressed and races out the door in a mad hurry, and whatever Will wanted gets done in a rush, but it does get done.

Boys will be boys

Boys are far more physical than girls and need to release all the excess energy that builds up from sitting too long. They have to go outside for a bit of rough and tumble. It's fun! Boys have fierce animal instincts that are with them from birth. It is a survival mechanism and their power. One way to guide them to use their energy constructively is through an organised physical activity like sport training or games involving teamwork.

The real me . . . or is it?

Anger turns us all into monsters, some of us more than others. Children need to recognise when they are having their buttons pushed, by whom and why. Parents like to think they are in control all the time but sometimes they lose control and that can be hard to handle. A typical example is having a new baby in the house and experiencing many long days and sleepless nights. All the baby seems to do is cry. Tension builds up and relationships become fragile. Tempers flare. All that is needed is to take a break, have a few good nights' sleep and give each other a lot of understanding, with plenty of loving and caring.

A good exercise for when tension is building up is to make a list of all the things and the people you resent. Look at how they make you feel and look at how they mirror things within yourself. You can only change yourself not others. So find ways to deal with the situation, forgive and move on.

When the bubble bursts

Jayne

Jayne's story teaches us how anger can be useful. Jayne came to me and poured her heart out—she needed to talk. She was crying and highly emotional. She wanted to share how she had experienced a horrendous childhood which led her to leave home at an early age. She came from a large family where sexual abuse was experienced by all the family. She married the first man she met hoping to escape her family, but the man she married turned out to be a criminal running from town to town.

At first the marriage was bearable, but then the beatings started and she was forced into sexual acts, not just with her husband but with others, and eventually she was forced into prostitution. Until, finally, she discovered her daughter was being sexually abused as well. All the pain and all the fear were transformed; suppressed anger raged within her. She took her daughter's hand and went for help and shelter.

Jayne and her daughter are now trying to lead a 'normal' life, trying to deal with what life has dealt them. Jayne tried to control her life and her emotions for too long, until the pain became too much. Her life had been a continual charade until she found out about her daughter's abuse. She didn't want her own children to go through what she had. Her own anger helped her to leave and now she is trying to rebuild a life for herself and her daughter.

Turning frustration and anger into positive action

Writing down all the things that make you angry and frustrated helps you to release and let go of pent up feelings. It makes you realise what you don't want in your life, and you become more aware of the things that cause your anger to erupt. It also helps you realise that sometimes when you are angry with your children you are experiencing redirected anger and frustration. It can help you understand why your children get angry and react the way they do.

What follows anger is regret—the guilt of what has been said and done—shame and self-reproach. Some children take anger personally and take it to heart. If they cannot cope with the situation they may run away, or take drugs or alcohol. They may experience severe anxiety and depression.

My son never threw a tantrum until he reached his teenage years. When my daughter threw a tantrum in our local shopping mall I just walked off. She soon caught me up. My youngest daughter throws tantrums all the time. She watches your reaction and plays on it. She'll be a great actress one day. Her trouble is she feels ashamed of herself. She throws a wobbly, regrets what she has done, and bursts into tears. One day at school the children were asked to write something about themselves. My daughter wrote how she doesn't like the way she storms off into her bedroom after shouting at people. Out of the mouths of babes!

Acknowledging how your children feel and why is half the battle won. Then by finding positive ways to deal with their problems you can win the war. How a situation is dealt with should determine your child's reaction. Every action has a reaction. Everyone is in control if they want to be, but if a situation gets out of hand people can get hurt. Many a cruel word is said in the heat of the moment.

Expression with clarity

Positive sayings to help your children with clear, positive communication

- I am honest and truthful to myself and others.
- I speak and express myself clearly and positively.
- I respect myself and others at all times.
- I express my anger in a way that doesn't harm myself or others.

Horse ride to freedom

A meditation to help release any hidden anger in your children

Lie down and get comfortable. Now gently close your eyes. Imagine a great big ball of sunlight right above your head. The ball of sunlight sends bright shining rays of light down on top of your head and you feel its warmth. The rays of light stream down your hair, across your shoulders and all the way down your arms to your precious little fingers. The warmth fills you as it streams down through your body, all the way down your legs to the end of each and every one of your precious little toes. You feel warm and safe.

Imagine a beautiful horse is standing right beside you. Climb up onto it and take the reins. You are riding the horse and as you do you notice how the wind is rushing through your hair brushing away any fears and worries you may have. You let them go. How fast are you going? Notice how you feel. You come to a big canyon where you stop and get off the horse. As you look out into the wide open space gather together all the thoughts and feelings you have about what is making you angry. When you have collected all your thoughts I want you to imagine yourself shouting them out as loud as you can and imagine the thoughts and feelings crashing against the walls of the canyon. See them leaving you now. Let go of everything that makes you angry now. When you have shouted as hard and as loud as you can, sit quiet and still and notice how you feel.

Any time you feel yourself getting angry and frustrated you can come back to this place to shout, release and let go of all that bothers you. You can do this as many times as you like. If you feel you have let go of all your feelings of anger you can open your eyes. When you are fully awake you will be relaxed and calm.

Suggested Australian Bush Flower Essences

To relieve anxiety: Dog Rose, Crowea
To restore inner balance: Jacaranda, Bush Fuchsia, Crowea
To lower high blood pressure: Crowea, Five Corners, Mountain Devil
To correct brain imbalances: Bush Fuchsia, Sun Dew, Isopogon
To alleviate depression: Kapok Bush, Flannel Flower, Wild Potato Bush, Red Grevillea
To relieve frustration: Old Man Banksia, Black-eyed Susan, Jacaranda, Sunshine Wattle, Red Grevillea
To express feelings: Flannel Flower
To release anger: Mountain Devil
To overcome shame: Billy Goat Plum

Parents' page

If any of your children are angry it can be very taxing on every member of the family. That's another reason to help your children deal with their anger and turn it into a positive emotion instead of a destructive one. Once again, communication is the key. When we communicate we understand how others feel. It is important to make a real effort to listen to what other people have to say. We may not agree with them but we must respect their feelings.

As I explained before, each family member has a right to their opinion as long as it doesn't hurt or harm another family member. Family meetings are excellent to sort through problems as they arise. It is a time for everyone to speak up and be heard. If your children feel angry about something this is a good time for the family to listen and find possible solutions.

Guidelines for family meetings

1. Set aside a suitable time for all family members to meet.
2. Allocate the time you want to spend together.
3. Ask for commitment and honesty and all promise that no judgements will be made about anyone.
4. Acknowledge each person's feelings and assessments even though you may not agree with them.
5. Note down family decisions and then monitor the changes.
6. Most importantly, listen—allow everyone to speak without interruption.
7. Be true to yourself.
8. Try to keep the meetings positive and always finish on a positive note.

Aromatherapy and Australian Bush Flower Essences can play a big part in clear, successful communication for yourself and your family. Use aromatherapy in all the rooms of the house for a calm and relaxed environment. The Australian Bush Flower Essences will bring clarity of mind and speech. Meditating as a family group will allow for free communication. Sharing your experiences together as a family is invaluable.

Clear, calm and collected—positive sayings to help you communicate effectively and positively

- I am able to communicate clearly.
- I am calm and relaxed in any situation and am able to act and react with precision.
- I am a loving caring person who is able to give and receive support in times of need.
- I can cope with any of life's challenges that may arise, efficiently and effectively.

The pyramid of love—a meditation to help you relax when your children are angry

Sit down or lie down and get comfortable. Now close your eyes. Imagine a fountain above your head. Golden droplets of water flow freely from the fountain, falling gently onto the top of your head. You feel the golden droplets flow down your head, across your shoulders, relaxing each and every muscle in your face and shoulders. They flow down your arms all the way to your fingers. You feel each muscle relax. You feel any tension being released, leaving your body, while the droplets flow down your torso. You become lighter as every muscle in your head, shoulders, arms and body relaxes. Droplets flow down your legs all the way to your feet.

Now imagine you are lying at the base of a pyramid. You notice swirls of green mist in the air all around you filling you with love. You are love. Feel it embrace you. Now the mist changes to a beautiful blue colour. As it changes colour you feel your throat chakra opening and you are able to communicate freely. The blue mist engulfs you and you are able to speak and listen with clarity and in a positive way.

The mist changes to a beautiful purple colour that swirls and swirls around you. You feel peace of mind as this colour fills your being, connecting you to the power of the universe. You are being guided along the right path. Now imagine you are connecting to your higher self. Feel the connection and acknowledge any thoughts you have now. Once again the mist changes to green and you are filled with an all-powerful love. If there is anything you would like guidance or help with ask your higher self now and listen for the answer.

When you are ready open your eyes. When you come out of this meditation you will be calm and relaxed. You are able to deal with other people in a positive and effective manner, one that will lead to a positive outcome.

Suggested Australian Bush Flower Essences

To relieve anxiety: Dog Rose, Crowea
To restore balance: Jacaranda, Bush Fuchsia, Crowea
To relieve frustration: Old Man Banksia, Black-eyed Susan, Jacaranda, Sunshine Wattle, Red Grevillea
To restore calm: Emergency Essence
To express feeling: Flannel Flower
To release anger: Mountain Devil
To overcome shame: Billy Goat Plum

The next chapter will help you cope in crisis situations that you may find yourself or one of your family members in. Hopefully the following information will help each one in your family deal with these situations successfully when they arise. Remember, you are never alone, so if you need help please refer to the resources section at the back of the book for the names and telephone numbers of organisations that can offer you assistance, or advice and support.

11
EATING DISORDERS

What we feed our mental, physical and spiritual body makes us who we are.

The previous chapters have looked at the foundations of raising children. Now we are going to examine some crisis situations you may encounter with your children, including signs to look for, what to do and how to deal with these extreme reactions or behaviours. Sometimes it is difficult as parents not to be over-protective with our children. So many things can go wrong, altering our lives just because of one person's actions or behaviour. It is important we keep communication open and be honest with our children so that we know what is going on in their lives without intruding.

Eating disorders affect many children every year. It is an increasing problem and one that we need to be well informed of. According to recent health statistics over half of all adolescent girls try to lose weight. Girls often feel that they are fat even though they are not, whereas many boys think that they are not big enough when they are.

The body is a temple—a priceless vehicle to house our soul and spirit. As you know, we come in different sizes, shapes and colours but each bodily form is just as precious as the next. How we treat our body is essential to our health, therefore, diet and exercise play a major role in maintaining good health and vitality.

Recent studies show that 90–95 per cent of people suffering from anorexia are female and they are most likely to be between 11 and 35 years of age. Children from affluent homes are prone to the illness, and a large percentage of anorexics become bulimic. Anorexia nervosa is diagnosed when a person loses about 15 percent of their body weight. Bulimia is thought to affect one in six students and usually strikes females aged between 15 and 24 years of age.

The tendency towards suffering from an eating disorder, including anorexia and compulsive eating, is believed to be formed by age 8 and in the case of bulimia by the age of 12.

So what causes children or teenagers to become anorexic, bulimic or compulsive eaters? As children become teenagers, they become very aware of how their bodies are changing and developing. Girls become aware of developing breasts, hips and thighs changing; measuring each ounce of fat that appears on their body in their teens. They compare lunches and discuss what is fattening with their friends. Teenagers constantly try to find what makes them different from everyone else. They are trying to make a good impression on others and will change their appearance in order to gain acceptance. Society today, especially through the media and fashion, shows the 'perfect' body as thin and waif-like, making children and teenagers with more body fat feel abnormal. Thinness gets equated with happiness! Some young people believe that if their bodies are not perfect they won't be accepted for who they are and they start dieting.

People suffering from anorexia or bulimia are obsessed with their weight and what they eat. According to the Centre for Eating Disorders, eating disorders are caused by an interaction of several factors which may include stress and lack of coping skills; traumatic situations and family problems; as well as outside influences, for instance, peers, the media and so on. People with anorexia may start dieting and not know how to stop. They are usually quite immature and seek to be more independent as well as needing to increase their sexual confidence. As they control what they eat, they get thinner and thinner, getting comments on how good they look which makes them want to carry on dieting to look even better. They become painfully thin and often are unable to see themselves as they really are. Tragically for some death is the final outcome.

On the other hand, people who suffer from bulimia often begin a diet, but the dieting causes them to have cravings for food and they then start bingeing. This causes them to feel out of control which lowers their self-esteem; they feel revolting and make themselves vomit or purge. Then they feel guilty, hate themselves and may get depressed. Their self-esteem and image suffers again and the cycle begins anew as they diet to try and improve their appearance. Bulimia is diagnosed when a sufferer has a minimum average of two episodes of binge eating a week for at least three months. Sufferers can consume up to around 12,000 calories in a relatively short period of time.

Compulsive eating affects males and females of all ages. Often these people just have a raging love affair with food. They eat in a frenzy and often they don't even really know what the food tastes like because of the quantity they have consumed. They lose the ability to connect hunger with food and their eating habits may replace relationships.

Both bulimic and compulsive eaters eat to numb their feelings while those with anorexia try very hard to not show their emotions. All three eating disorders have deep-seated emotional origins that need to be identified and dealt with.

Sufferers of anorexia and bulimia starve their bodies of vital nutrients and the uncontrollable desire to continue the obsession continues with a drive so powerful it overwhelms them and clouds their judgement and behaviour.

Am I attractive enough?

I suffered from anorexia at the age 19, going from 52 kg down to 40 kg. I was one of the lucky ones who saw the light and realised what I was doing to myself. Unfortunately not too many children have that experience. The story that follows is similar to my own and is probably the same for many people with this terrible disease.

Angie

Angie's engagement of two years was failing. She was living in a foreign country far from home and her fiancÈ travelled with his work, leaving her alone most of the time. She began to lose interest in her food because her heart was breaking and she felt lost. She longed for attention.

As she began to lose weight she became obsessed with trying to look better, not realising she was getting too thin. She drank laxative tea and made excuses not to eat with others. She made herself scarce at meal times and started a rigorous exercise programme. As her outfits got bigger on her she secretly took the seams in so no one would notice. A couple of times she was picked up off the pavement and taken to hospital because she had collapsed from lack of energy and iron deficiency.

People started to comment on Angie's weight loss but she just couldn't see it; she still looked fat in the mirror. The engagement was finally broken off and luckily for Angie she ended up back at home with her parents who were devastated by Angie's appearance and the state of her health. They got medical help immediately and Angie was put on a special programme to help rebuild her life.

Thanks to her parents, Angie survived her ordeal. Today she is a healthy mother of two, but she still lives with the nagging feeling she doesn't look good enough. The main physical problems she faces now have to do with her teeth. Due to her poor diet she has lost many teeth and even now she is undergoing treatment on the bone structure of her jaws to keep the teeth she has.

There are many factors that cause eating disorders including both external influences and inner conflicts. The patterns of these disorders have already been learnt before a child's teenage years and remain undetected until triggered by the right stimulus. High achievers and perfectionists seem more prone to suffer from an eating disorder.

According to the Centre for Eating Disorders, sufferers of anorexia are often described as obsessive, deceitful, hysterical, emotional, immature, moody, perfectionists, competitive, self critical, controlled, compulsive, anxious, and approval seeking. Bulimic and compulsive eaters are often described as: compulsive, emotionally unstable, uncontrolled, depressed, impulsive and deceitful. They are often caught stealing food because of the amounts they consume.

Anorexia—warning signs

Does your child have an obsession with weight, often thinking of herself as being fat or overweight? Does she make excuses not to be around at meal times or tell people she is not hungry? Does she eat alone and hide food or throw food away? Is she frightened of putting on weight? Does she have a fear of being out of control that makes her anxious and she behaves erratically? Has she taken on a rigorous exercise programme? Does she use laxatives? Have you noticed any major weight loss?

If you have answered 'yes' to any of the questions above, your child could be in danger. The following list describes further symptoms and effects of anorexia nervosa:

- insomnia
- low self-esteem

- conversations about dieting, weight loss and gain and food
- loss of or erratic menstruation cycle (females)
- poor concentration or the appearance that their judgement is clouded
- sensitivity to the cold
- mood swings, depression, emotionally unbalanced
- change in personality
- isolation from relationships
- dizziness
- skin tone changes and becomes dry and lined—even in young children
- hair looks dull and has lost its lustre
- cuts and wounds take a long time to heal
- low blood pressure
- soft downy hair over body especially the hands, face and back.

Does your child exhibit any of these signs and symptoms?

Bulimia—warning signs

Does your child lose control when it comes to food? Does your child binge on high fat, sweet, or rich foods? Have you noticed him making many trips to the bathroom after eating? Does she use laxatives? Has he recently begun a vigorous exercise programme to combat weight gain? If this describes your child's behaviour, your child could be bulimic. The following list describes further symptoms and effects of bulimia:

- low self-esteem
- conversations about dieting, weight loss or weight gain and food
- weighs a little more than the average weight for their height

- sore throat and stomach from vomiting
- poor teeth due to frequent vomiting
- suffers mood swings, has signs of depression, or is emotionally unbalanced
- exhibits changes in personality
- isolation from relationships
- suffers from pins and needles in the limbs
- has had convulsions
- has been diagnosed with anaemia
- has hair loss
- has been diagnosed with heart or kidney damage due to a lack of potassium in the diet
- skin has a bloated, blotched appearance
- suffers soreness around the anus
- suffers from oedema (fluid retention)
- has abdominal swelling.

Does your child exhibit any of these signs?

Compulsive eaters—warning signs

Is your child overweight? Does she often seem out of breath? Does she lack energy? Have you asked her doctor or school nurse to check if she has higher blood pressure than normal for her age? Compulsive eaters often suffer from diabetes or gall bladder disease. Other signs to be aware of are a tendency towards depression, increased metabolism and lack of self-control. Be warned—compulsive eaters are secretive! You'll find empty packets and lolly wrappers around their room, hidden away, or stuffed in their pockets. They often eat only small amounts in public but put on weight.

Because of the extra strain on the body most compulsive eaters have a shorter life expectancy than is normal for their age. If left untreated even the less significant symptoms can become very serious, both physically and mentally, or even fatal. Children who suffer from eating disorders tend to become lonely and withdrawn. They become frightened about what people may think or say about them, but in almost every case they want someone to help them recover. Usually they are simply too scared to ask for help. If any of your children are suffering from an eating disorder seek help as soon as possible; early intervention is essential. Please see the resources list at the back of the book.

I am beautiful

Positive sayings to help rebuild a broken soul

- I am beautiful inside and out and love fills my heart.
- I am confident in everything I do and say.
- I live in the present.
- My body and mind receive the very best nourishment for them to function effectively and successfully, allowing me to achieve all I set out to.

I am beautiful—I am me

A meditation to help your children to see how beautiful they really are

Get really comfortable—either sit down or lie down. Now close your eyes. Imagine a golden light shining down from the sky, beaming right down onto the top of your head. As it flows down lots of tiny multi-coloured rainbows sprinkle down over your head, flashing all the way through your body. See how it makes your body glitter and shine. Colours of every kind sparkle and flash up and down your body filling you with love. Feel your body as it glows with warmth.

Imagine you are in a cocoon of silky soft tissue that holds

you safe and warm. As you lie here you feel the rainbow's light shining from within you, out through your body, through the silk of the cocoon and out into the world. Everything around you looks beautiful and fresh. You want to reach out and touch it. The silk tissue slowly begins to unravel and you feel yourself being set free. Go as slowly or as quickly as you wish, making sure you are completely free of the silk tissue. You are standing firm upon the ground, strong and well balanced. The rainbows continue to shine out from within you and when you look down at your body you can see an amazing array of colours just swirling in and out of your body. As they swirl out they make the world around you brighter. When they swirl in you feel energy filling your heart, mind and soul. Suddenly you notice many people around you who love and care for you. Greet them now in a way you feel comfortable with. When you have greeted them ask them to help you put your life back in order. Whether you need support, or lots of love and care, whatever it is ask them now. Speak clearly and with confidence. Now ask them how you can help them to help you. Listen to what they have to say.

When you have finished talking you can walk to one of your favourite places, where you feel calm, relaxed and safe. You can rest here until you need to speak to your friends again. You have shed your cocoon and you are truly a beautiful creature who is blossoming every minute of every day. Feel your beauty both inside and out and let it shine for everyone to see. I am leaving you here and when you feel comfortable you can open your eyes.

Suggested Australian Bush Flower Essences

To relieve anxiety: Dog Rose, Crowea
To help treat appetite disorders: Dog Rose, Paw Paw, Crowea, Five Corners, Bluebell
To restore balance: Jacaranda, Bush Fuchsia, Crowea

To deal with low blood pressure: Southern Cross, Kapok Bush, Five Corners

To help treat bulimia: Billy Goat Plum, Grey Spider Flower, Five Corners

To combat dehydration: She Oak

To overcome depression: Kapok Bush, Flannel Flower, Wild Potato Bush, Red Grevillea

To help with being overweight: Old Man Banksia, Wild Potato Bush, Mulla Mulla, Dog Rose, Fringed Violet

Parents' page

Blaming yourself for what is happening to your children does not help anyone. You will experience many difficult emotions such as anger, anxiety, guilt and stress, while your children will be fighting for a balance between dependence and independence. Because of the stresses involved it is normal for one parent in a two-parent family to withdraw from the situation but, hopefully, you and your partner will be able to work through this challenge together. Remember there is help and support all around you.

Children with eating disorders may have been suffering a long time before their parents want to acknowledge that there is a problem. If you have been slow to discover your child's eating disorder, once you overcome any feelings of shame, there is much you can do to help your children recover.

When you discover there is a problem, the first step is to communicate your fears with your children openly and honestly. Describe your feelings to them without any criticism, accusations or blame. Depending on the type of relationship you have with your children, and whether they are used to open communication, they may react angrily or aggressively; they may deny any such action; they may ignore you or they may ask for help. It is important that you stay calm, patient, loving and supportive during the whole recovery process.

Communicate and listen to your children and encourage them along their new path.

If you suspect your children are suffering from an eating disorder

1. Deal with it as soon as you suspect anything by talking to your children openly and honestly.
2. Seek medical advice and a clear diagnosis from a professional.
3. Follow professional advice which may include counselling, psychiatric help, medication and education about eating habits.
4. Have your children's teeth checked by a dentist. Poor dietary habits and vomiting may have damaged their teeth.
5. Have a look at your own eating habits and change them too if necessary.

Once your children have agreed to go to the doctor make sure they keep the appointment. You might like to ask your doctor some of the following questions:

- Is there someone that specialises in eating disorders in your area that can help?
- Where are self-help and support groups located?
- Where can you get more information to help educate family members?
- Can you give me a referral to a professional or organisation that can be of help?

In the case of severe anorexia the sufferer may need hospitalisation to receive help for recovery. Your doctor may suggest psychotherapy or counselling to help the sufferer's mental wellbeing. The Centre for Eating Disorders warns that many sufferers have to be readmitted to hospital because the underlying problems may not have been totally resolved.

Many bulimic and compulsive eaters usually prefer to have outpatient treatment or attend self-help groups in which they can progress at their own pace. Self-help groups provide encouragement and education and help sufferers acknowledge their particular problem, which is half the battle.

All sufferers need to work at assessing and accepting emotions, feelings and needs. They must build a good healthy self-esteem and self-image. Make food and eating something 'normal' and not something to be disliked, or used.

How can you help your child get their life back on track?

Here are suggestions from various hospitals and centres that specialise in eating disorders:

1. Encourage your children to see a therapist.
2. Allow them to see the therapist alone and don't pry into what has been said.
3. Don't make an issue about food or weight and be flexible with eating habits.
4. Don't punish them for being ill—they're already punishing themselves.
5. Get them to take responsibility for their actions.
6. Learn to deal effectively with the conflict—don't criticise the child, only the action.
7. Don't allow them to manipulate any given situation.
8. Use a reward system to encourage more acceptable behaviour.
9. Look after your own relationships. This can cause major stress within the family so find ways to reduce stress and take time out for yourself and your partner.
10. The whole family can attend self-help groups for counselling

Some therapists recommend that bulimic or compulsive eaters keep a journal listing the time, date, food or drink item consumed; why they ate at that time and how it made them feel (guilty, angry, etc.); the binge time and date; whether they vomited, purged or exercised and how they feel now. They should begin to fill in the journal after every meal or snack—they must be totally honest. (It is for their benefit and they may like to keep it secret.) They should write down all their fears, worries and emotions, for instance, what makes them angry and so on. After a week or two they should look back through their journal to identify patterns in their behaviour.

The following questions are a guide to help your children reflect on their journal writing exercise and get the most benefit from it.

- What foods do I crave?
- How often do I eat these foods and why?
- When do my binges start—is there a special time?
- Is there a time when I exercise more?
- Am I being honest in my journal? Is what I write true?
- What things are causing my stress and are they being dealt with appropriately?

Addressing these questions will help the bulimic or compulsive eater to become more controlled and responsible. Remember that once the sufferer has committed themselves to seeking help it is up to them to heal themselves. It won't be easy or quick. The road to recovery requires love, support, care, courage and strength from everyone.

All of the therapies described in this book will be of tremendous benefit to everyone in the family. I do suggest that you are flexible in the use of these therapies and any others you try, if your children find it difficult to relate to them. But medical help is essential for sufferers of eating disorders.

The carer—positive sayings to help you cope with this crisis

- I am a wonderful parent for my children.
- When I experience pangs of anger, anxiousness, guilt or

stress I am able to control and express my feelings in a positive, calm, meaningful way.

- I have all the people I need to help me face and deal with any challenges life has given me. I am always giving and receiving love. I am love.
- I am a good communicator. I speak with clarity and am positive.

Talking with your child—a meditation to help you communicate with a child who may be suffering from an eating disorder

Lie or sit down in a comfortable position and gently close your eyes. Now take three long deep breaths, breathing in slowly and deeply, and breathing out hard and strong. As you breathe in, you feel yourself becoming more and more relaxed and as you breathe out let go of anything that has been worrying you. Release all your feelings and emotions and let go. Lie here quiet and still for a couple of minutes. Now imagine you are being filled with love; so much love that you can feel it in every part of your body. It is warming you and filling you more and more until you can feel love oozing out through the pores in your skin. You look up and see a golden sun shining brightly in the sky, its rays beating down on the ground. The sky is blue, without a cloud in sight.

Now you are walking. Notice how you are walking. Are you walking quickly or slowly? How is your body moving? Is it moving confidently or are you shaky? Whatever way you were walking, you walk now with strong steps placing your feet firmly on the ground, gripping the earth with courage and direction. Feel your body fill with confidence and self-assurance. As you walk, shed any remaining fears, worries or negative emotions by the wayside—leave them there. Let them go.

Up ahead you meet your child. Acknowledge your child the best way you can. As you stand here with your child start talking with them. Let them know how you feel, openly and honestly. Say what you have to say then release and let go. Trust the universe to help serve your best interests and those of your child. Now ask your child what they would like to say to you and listen to the reply.

When you have finished talking with your child slowly open your eyes and write down everything you have experienced. You may never share this experience with your child, but ask and look for guidance and signs to help you with your child. Know now that you are a wonderful human being and a wonderful parent. Everything that happens within your life happens for a reason. Seek the positive and act accordingly.

Suggested Australian Bush Flower Essences

To relieve anxiety: Dog Rose, Crowea
To overcome depression: Kapok Bush, Flannel Flower, Wild Potato Bush, Red Grevillea
To deal with frustration: Old Man Banksia, Black-eyed Susan, Jacaranda, Sunshine Wattle, Red Grevillea

Eating disorders are usually a form of self-abuse. In the next chapter we are going to find ways to cope and to heal when children have had intellectual, emotional, spiritual, sexual or physical abuse inflicted upon them.

12
CHILD ABUSE

Each soul has a spirit that must light every corner of the universe with its beauty and magnificence.

The used and abused

As I explained in the previous chapter on eating disorders, this chapter deals with abuse that is inflicted from outside the victims rather than from within as in eating disorder sufferers. This chapter deals with abuse that will undermine any of the foundations laid out in this book, so the fundamentals will need to be rebuilt.

Whether intellectual, emotional, spiritual, sexual or physical abuse, all are harmful to the body, mind and soul. Boundaries have been broken and children feel unsafe, or always on their guard. If your children mention anything to do with abuse take it seriously and take the time to listen to them—children do not make up stories about abusive situations. Take some form of action. Abuse may have been going on for many years and quite often there is more than one person being abused within the household. Children in this situation are often threatened by the perpetrator to such a degree that they feel they can never tell anyone what is going on and many live their lives in denial, coping with the trauma by forgetting what has happened. Quite often children will not disclose their terrible trauma until an event like separation, divorce, a death or a birthday triggers something inside them to finally say no more!

Many of these children try to escape by turning to the streets. Others form negative addictions by turning to drugs or alcohol. Many become anorexic as a way of making themselves seem unattractive. Some try self-mutilation for the same reason and, tragically, some children commit suicide because the pain is just too much to bear. If adults, as children, have suppressed their feelings and emotions and have never told anyone what has happened they may become workaholics to keep the memories from coming forward. Many abused adults become abusers. Whatever age, abused people try to maintain their lives by controlling every part, which can be obsessive. Disclosing to another person what they have been through is extremely frightening and stressful so if you have any idea someone may be the victim of abuse seek professional help straight away.

One young girl I helped to treat carried her guilt around for nineteen years before she sought help. She had been abused by her father and her brothers. She chose inner child work to help her regain the childhood she had blotted out. She also used inner child therapies to help her find herself. Although the experience was extremely painful, she was able to release many feelings and emotions she had pushed deep down inside herself and was able to move on with her life.

These children experience very strong emotions. While they are still being abused their behaviour may seem very bizarre and out of character at times. They will experience anger, guilt, pain, fear, hate, hurt and resentment. These children are survivors and will carry their abuse for the rest of their lives. It is a heavy load for anyone to bear. What they have experienced is real. They need to know that the abuse they have experienced is not their fault. In their relationships with non-abusers, they may stand back, be reserved or secretive giving little away, or they may find it difficult to know whom to trust.

We cannot 'fix' abused children. They must find a working way to solve the conflicts and pain of their inner and outer being. All we can do as parents is to love and support them. We can guide them, making sure we don't try and push too hard—they have been pushed one too many times already. Although it may be difficult for us as their supporters we have to allow them to cry, or let them shout and scream. Allow them to feel the pain, the loneliness, the anger and the grief. These children will not like the person that they are—allow them that. They need to rebuild their self-esteem and feel safe again.

Children who have been victims of abuse need reassurance. They need to understand that self-destructive behaviour is not a way out of their dilemma. While they are going through the healing process it is important their lives are kept fairly simple and on an even keel. They should not make any rash decisions. Also as a parent you need to be able to take the time to listen to them and to be aware of any behavioural changes. This can be very tiring for you and your family members.

Once children have gone through the initial process and are further down the track, it is often advisable for them to try and forgive the abuser. The reasoning behind this is that the act of forgiveness:

- helps to heal the emotions.
- helps the abused to remember and let go rather than suppressing their thoughts and feelings.
- helps them to understand that it is not their fault.
- helps build trust in new or existing relationships—remember these children have hidden so much from so many people.
- allows the abused to vent their anger. Anger can be very destructive and can undermine their sense of self. To bring the anger out into the open releases so much.

- allows them to face the abuser if they want to without the fear of reprisals and, if there are reprisals, lets them deal with these positively.

Many abused children have problems forming close relationships. It may be years before an abused child will allow any recollection of the abuse and this can cause problems, particularly if a child's memory is suddenly triggered when they are in a new relationship. Many of these children are caught up in abusive cycles. All it takes is a trigger and they act either in accordance with what has been taught or they rebel. All we can do is to teach our children to be open and honest with us. Many parents have little idea what is happening to their children when they are separated from them; for example, while they are at work, out shopping, and so on.

One family I helped had 'friends' who were close to the whole family. They did everything together: visited one another, came for barbecues, even went on holidays together; but eventually it was discovered that their friends—adults—were connected to a group of people who wanted to 'play' with children. Needless to say, the association was broken off very quickly.

Let your children know it is okay to say no to anyone. Let them know it is safe to talk to you. If they can't talk to you, get help, find a counsellor who has specialised in this field. Please see the reference section at the back of the book.

There are some things children can do to help themselves and these include:

1. Meditating and learning deep breathing exercises.
2. Finding someone they feel safe with that they can talk to.
3. Identifying places and people they feel safe with—this lowers anxiety and reduces the likelihood of panic attacks.
4. Giving themselves the time and the space to feel and express their emotions.
5. Going to self-esteem classes.

Warning signs to look for include:

- bed wetting
- changes in sleeping habits
- changes in behaviour or erratic behaviour
- low self-esteem or always putting themselves down
- fear of going to certain places or meeting certain people
- loss of weight
- causing harm to themselves.

Courage talk

Positive sayings to help strengthen your children and build their sense of personal power

- All the feelings and emotions arising within me are okay. I am turning each one into a positive action now.
- I am a beautiful and wonderful person both inside and out.
- I have the strength and the courage to face and deal with everything my life is presenting to me now. I have love, care and support all around me at all times.
- I have the courage to speak my mind and release and let go of all the hurt, pain and anger inside me. I speak with a strong, clear voice and people listen to me.

Balloon ride to safety

A meditation to take your children to a place where they can let all their feelings and emotions go without fear of repercussions

Lie down and get really comfortable. Now gently close your eyes. As you lie here quiet and still take three long, slow, deep breaths. As you breathe in hold your breath to the count of three and do the same as you breathe out. Just above your head is a beautiful, bright, shining star. See it twinkle and glow. Watch the star as it starts shooting rays of white light down over the top of your head. Feel the white light gently cover you. Feel the rays of light gently move down your hair and your head to your neck. These rays of light bring every part of you alive and you are full of energy. Feel the rays move across your shoulders and down your arms, all the way down to each and every one of your fingers. Again feel the energy they fill you with. Bright sparks of energy move down through your chest area, releasing and letting go of any tightness you may be experiencing. Then down through your stomach area, again releasing any tension or pain there. The rays of light flow down through the rest of your body all the way down your legs to the end of each and every one of your toes.

Now you are going on a balloon ride so imagine yourself opening the door to the basket that will hold you safe. Above you the big brightly coloured balloon sways gently in the breeze. When you are ready, let your balloon take off from the ground. Can you feel yourself gently float up in the air? As you float along in the bright blue sky you look down and see your world below you. You pass green fields, trees full of birds, lakes with little boats on them. Take in all the beauty of nature you can see. Listen to the noises around you. You are part of this beauty. You are one of nature's gifts.

You are floating across a great dam full of blue water. Gather all the thoughts and feelings you have about the things that have made you angry or have caused you pain. Once you have got them all together put them in one of the sandbags sitting at your feet. Put all of these feelings and thoughts in the sandbag and throw the bag over the side of your balloon and watch as it falls through the air, splashing into the blue water of the dam. Watch it as it sinks to the bottom of the water, gone forever. As you have gotten rid of the bag of sand the balloon suddenly feels lighter. You feel yourself soaring high into the sky—as free as a bird. You are now at peace. You are quiet and still.

A bird comes to rest on the side of the basket you are standing in. This bird is your friend and it asks you to tell it anything you want to. Take a few moments to talk to this bird about anything you wish it to know. Know now that anything you tell this bird is in strictest confidence. The bird is here for you to release and let go of your inner self. Speak honestly and be true to yourself. When you have shared all you wish to tell the bird thank it and send it away with love. The bird flies away from you but you can call on it at any time.

Your balloon comes in to land safely on the ground. Step out onto the ground and stand by the balloon. Feel the ground beneath your feet and imagine a bright light coming down from the sky, going through your head and down your back all the way down to the ground. It is like a rod linking you to both the sky and the ground; feel it balance you and steady you; feel its strength as it holds you firm.

When you are ready open your eyes and take a few moments to understand how you feel. If you want to, write down some of the things you have experienced on your journey. Keep a record of how you progress each time you go on your journey. You may like to vary the places you go in your hot-air balloon but you can come here any time for peace of mind.

Suggested Australian Bush Flower Essences

To overcome addictions: Bottlebrush, Waratah, Red Lily, Sundew, Flannel Flower, Five Corners

To deal with anxiety: Dog Rose, Crowea

To overcome depression: Kapok Bush, Flannel Flower, Wild Potato Bush, Red Grevillea

To overcome the fear of touch: Billy Goat Plum, Wisteria, Red Helmet, Flannel Flower

To end nervousness: Dog Rose, Black-eyed Susan, Jacaranda, Emergency Essence
To cope with shock: Emergency Essence, Fringed Violet

Parents' page

Having any kind of information that leads you to believe your children are being mentally or physically abused will come as a shock to you. It is important that you act on the information straight away—I cannot emphasise that enough. Yes, the road ahead of you may be daunting and scary—it may even change your life—but for the sake of your children you have to do something about it. It is up to you to listen to the victims and heed what is said. Get professional help as soon as possible. Understand that this may be a long and painful time for all of you but it is the path you must take. The best way to defeat this problem is to face it, deal with it and let your lives move on. That doesn't mean to say forget it and pretend it never happened, but acknowledge it and work through it in a way you are all comfortable with.

Some things you can do to protect and help heal your children

1. Teach them to say no—to stand up for their own beliefs.
2. Listen to them and don't take their feelings and thoughts lightheartedly—they are real!
3. Get professional help for your children—find people they can talk to when the going gets rough—teach them to ask for help. Give them a list of people they can contact at any time, and place it in their purse or wallet.
4. Educate yourself about abuse and trauma.
5. Don't ask or wait for proof.
6. Let them live in the here and now because it's all they can deal with when they are in the process of healing.

7. Get help for yourself—it's not an easy road to walk and you don't have to do it alone either.
8. Take time for yourself.
9. Make sure both or all of you are in a safe environment.
10. Through the help of a children's counsellor help your children establish a new way of living, setting new boundaries and new ways of thinking.

Prayer and meditation will help a great deal in this situation. Both will give a sense of relief and release. A few sessions with Kinergetics will help to break the cycle that has been formed and will help with ways of moving on with life. The use of essential oils and Australian Bush Flower Essences on a daily basis will also help relieve feelings and emotions.

I am strong and I have courage to succeed—positive sayings to help you cope

- I have the strength and the courage to deal with anything for myself or my family.
- I am able to speak with clarity and precision, making all the right decisions at the right time for everyone involved.
- I am kind, sensitive and firm in all I do. I am protected at all times from anything or anyone that may want to harm me mentally or physically.
- I know my own limits and my boundaries and these keep me safe and protect me at all times.

Forgiveness—a meditation to help you forgive the person who has caused you or your children pain
(You may want to adapt this meditation for your children.)

Lie or sit down and get really comfortable. Now close your eyes. Take three long, deep, slow breaths. Feel the air flow into your body and out again. Just relax. A magnificent golden light is streaming down onto your head, spreading down your neck, across your shoulders and all the way down your arms to the end of your fingers. The golden light shimmers as it flows down through your body, filling every part of you. See how it glows strongly around your heart area. Your heart glows. The golden light flows freely and swiftly down your legs, all the way to each and every one of your toes. Imagine a great big bubble forming all around you. The filmy bubble encloses you and makes you feel safe and secure. The air inside your bubble turns a beautiful green colour and you feel love engulf you. Let the love soak into your body now. This love is for you—you are love.

As you lie or sit here imagine the person you need to speak to drawing near. If you don't want to look at them that's okay, just sense their presence here with you now, and understand that you are safe and protected by the bubble that surrounds you. There is no need to feel any fear or anxiety. Relax and continue to absorb the green light that fills your bubble.

As you sense this person before you, take the time to say all the things you wish to say to them; these may be angry statements but take the time now to let this person know your feelings and emotions. Let them all out—speak freely and honestly knowing you are safe and secure. Love surrounds you. If you need to shout—shout. If you need to cry—cry. You are safe.

When you have said all you needed to say to this person take the time now to forgive the person before you. It may be hard but say, 'I forgive you for what you have done.' If it is hard for you to do, try whispering it quietly under your breath. The more you do this meditation the easier it will be to say, 'I forgive you.'

When you are ready, let this person walk away from you. Feel confident within yourself that you are okay. The love still flows into your body—feel it. When you are ready you open your eyes. Know now you have released and let go and still given and received love. You are truly a wonderful human being. You are now ready to move on.

Suggested Australian Bush Flower Essences

To deal with anxiety: Dog Rose, Crowea
To overcome depression: Kapok Bush, Flannel Flower, Wild Potato Bush, Red Grevillea
To end nervousness: Dog Rose, Black-eyed Susan, Jacaranda, Emergency Essence
To cope with shock: Emergency Essence, Fringed Violet

In the next chapter we are going to examine guilt and grief. These emotions are very strong and are closely connected to the last few chapters.

13
GUILT AND GRIEF

Grief is ours alone. How long we hold onto the pain is our choice.

As we have discovered in previous chapters, there are challenges we must meet on our journey through life. How we react to situations can determine how we fare in life. In this chapter we are going to look at how guilt and grief affect us and our families.

However much we wish to let go of one another, each person we meet remains a part of our memories. Whether we lose a loved one through death, separation or divorce, the pain and anguish, the seesaw of other emotions, such as the fear of change accompanying the loss, comes as a blow to our self-esteem and confidence, making us question our own self-worth and purpose. We have to decide whether we will wallow in our guilt, grief or self pity or pick ourselves up and live life the best way we can. We can stop putting up barriers that make us scared, cold and angry. We can rebuild our lives. Through tragedy and sorrow we can discover an inner strength we didn't know we had and learn from the experience.

The price of equality

Family life as we know it today is very different from the past. The close knit family is a thing of the past in many communities today, as family members take flight, seeking a home somewhere in the world that suits their dreams and wishes rather than staying in the small community or living just down the road from mum and dad, calling in every day for morning tea and the comfort of family life.

For some mothers the decision to go back to work or have a career outside the home is made for their own pleasure and to gain a greater sense of achievement, finishing a goal that was put on hold until the children were old enough.

Family life has to be adjusted to create the most functional and successful way of life and accommodate each individual. Children have to become more independent, taking more responsibility for what they do. They may also have to attend more before- and after-school care. Some children enjoy their newfound freedom and the quality time that their parents give them, while others suffer from lack of attention with a need for parental guidance and company, a cuddle and a kiss.

Spouses have to re-adjust to their partners not being around to share the household chores and duties all the time. They may have to put up with late nights at the office and coming home with extra work because it is the end of the month again. Some partners have to contend with a fear of competition, a feeling that their spouses may be more successful in business than they are. For many men their sense of purpose has been pulled away from under their feet, leaving them reeling. But some men love the change in lifestyle. They are following dreams they never expected to realise until they retired. Some of these changes have taken the pressure off men, allowing them to get in touch with their feelings and emotions and giving them a greater sense of freedom.

The price of equality has come dearly for many couples as

divorce or separation become more common, leaving a trail of disillusionment and scattered dreams.

Graham and Louise, a couple I know, had always worked towards their family goals together. Before having children they decided that Louise would stay home while the children were young and Graham would support the family financially as best he could. Before they had children they both worked very hard to get the things they wanted for their family including a nice home, a car, and they took holidays twice a year.

When Louise was eight months pregnant she left her job and took a couple of courses in counselling. When the children were older she decided to set up her own counselling practice. While the children were still young life had not been as easy as Graham and Louise had hoped. They were only living on one wage but Graham worked as hard as he could to give the family everything they needed. When Louise set up her practice it was an instant success and she started spending more and more time away from home. This affected the household in many ways. The children had to take public transport to and from school and their various extra-curricular activities. The evening meal was often late or rushed, and Graham felt left out and got very uptight thinking that perhaps he wasn't a good enough father and husband, while Louise was constantly tired.

Although the family adjusted to Louise going out to work, she was still doing as much around the house as she had before opening her practice. She felt overloaded and her health began to suffer. Louise was enjoying her work but her home life appeared to be crumbling. She believed her family was not supporting or helping her. Finally she decided enough was enough. After long arguments and much stress within the family she decided to separate from her husband. She felt she could cope much better on her own with the children and lead the life she wanted.

Graham and Louise's story is just one example of a family

under stress, but their story illustrates how jealousy, anger, frustration, hurt egos, a damaged pride and a sense of loss affect all the family. And underpinning all these emotions are guilt and grief—natural reactions to change.

Children have to cope with role changes within the family, which can be a difficult and confusing time at any age. Many people find that through changes in their career and lifestyle their personality changes and their partner can feel that the spouse they married is not the same person any more. Unless the family can adjust, divorce or separation becomes inevitable.

Children of divorced parents

Children of divorced parents tend to sabotage their own relationships before they have properly begun because they don't want to get attached to someone they fear they will lose later on. They find commitment hard, always wanting to be in control of their lives. Children in these situations need to know it is okay to form relationships and trust in everything that happens to them.

Coping with loss

Losing a family member is much the same whether we lose them through separation or divorce. We grieve for the loss of that relationship. Our feelings of helplessness turn to shock, denial, then anger and finally guilt and our Pandora's box of emotions overflows. Remember that the person, child or pet you have lost is in your heart forever. Your memories cannot be taken away. Having experienced the loss of my grandparents, of whom I was very fond, the loss of friends, and the loss of my youngest brother, and seeing my husband have so many terrible accidents, helped me to realise how fragile life is.

Sometimes we take life for granted, but we are reminded that it is short and to make the most of it.

Why do we wait to fulfil our dreams or those of our children until we are given six months to live? Every minute is precious, especially every minute we spend with our children—don't waste time! Most parents know what it is like to see their children go through illnesses, and some parents have to accept their children will not recover. I have seen parents who know they will lose their child, spending hours and hours with their loved one, trying to make the time they have left a little better. Many people experience anger as the death of a loved one grows near. They ask themselves what more can be done? When finally the family accepts their loss they experience a sense of peace.

I sat with my brother until he passed on and I still thank God today for allowing me to be there. It was wonderful to see the calmness come over him and it put my mind at rest to know he was at peace. I have met many people who have also had this experience and each one says the same thing. One man I spoke to said he had felt like crying leading up to his son's death, but when the time came he felt a presence sweep over him, calming him.

Coming to terms with a past relationship takes time. The heart is heavy and hurts, the mind is numbed and the body is usually starved of proper nourishment to keep it going. We doubt that we can ever form a new relationship again. And if someone new walks into our lives to step into the shoes of someone we lost, new doubts and fears arrive.

If you feel bad, have you thought about how your children feel about losing a sibling or a parent through death, separation or divorce?

According to the Holmes-Rahe Social Adjustment Scale, separation and divorce are the most stressful situations to be in and for many the struggle to cope with the loss is emotionally draining. The death of a loved one is the next most stressful situation.

When a marriage or relationship is severed or breaks down, waves of grief, guilt and anger affect everyone involved, including the children. Children going through grief and loss tend not to show their pain instantly. Sometimes it appears later when things have calmed down.

Children who are trying to cope with loss or grief may be aggressive or angry towards siblings, parents and animals, or even their toys. They may act younger than they are, needing more attention than usual or they may hide their sadness by doing more school work, or involving themselves in activities more than usual. They may even try to look after someone weaker than themselves. Often they seem to have poor concentration and daydream, or are 'off with the fairies'.

You can help your children through this stressful period in their life using communication. Listening to your children express how they feel is the key to everything you do. Regardless of what is going on, or how you feel, the doors to communication need to be open night and day. Communication lets everyone know where they stand, so honesty is important.

Each one of us has a role to play in our family team but if the rapport, respect and communication break down the whole family fragments, shattering into individual players who only join in when they feel like it. Children have their own points of view very early in life and their thoughts are important. They need to know their role in the family is important and that their thoughts and feelings are valid.

Children and adults alike need reassurance, and the spoken word and the action are imperative in rebuilding confidence and self-esteem. Families are like sports teams, only they are playing the game of life but, as with any team under stress, sometimes players have to go and find another team to play for, have time out for injury, or just find another home ground. If a team loses a player then they have the choice to bring in a reserve, another player to fill the place, not as a replacement but to help keep the team working the way it wants to.

Children's perceptions of relationships

In a lot of the marriages I have seen fall apart the children are the reflection of what is going on in their parents' lives. Children see, hear and sense everything in their parents' relationships. They know when things aren't right, especially when they see or hear their parents' disagreements. As they see the two people they love in conflict with each other they question their own position, their own beliefs, even their own value. Their self-esteem suffers as they feel they are the only person in the world this is happening to. Some children take the role of a 'marriage fixer', taking on added responsibility and carrying the guilt of everything that has happened on their own shoulders. Some children try to be extra good, while others play up, thinking that perhaps if they act this way mum and dad will stay together. One of the first things my children were concerned about was how they would tell other people their parents were separated and what would the other children in school think about it. After talking with a few of their friends, they discovered that many children were from single-parent families or blended families. Some children try to play the matchmaker, creating situations where their parents can be brought back together. Others play one parent off against the other to get the things they want. If possible both parents need to communicate, and join together to show a united front even though they are living apart.

Stepping back into the limelight

Caroline

Caroline was married for 20 years before her marriage ended. She was amazed at the reactions of some of her friends. They stopped inviting her to dinner parties and treated her as though she was a threat, an outsider. Caroline was dumped by her friends because of insecurities and conflicts her friends faced in their own marriages. Caroline had found the strength and conviction to move on from her broken marriage. Perhaps what her friends saw in Caroline was too much for them to bear. It could have been very easy for Caroline to sit at home feeling sorry for herself, and some days she did just that. Mostly she worked very hard on herself, searching for answers to questions about where she was going and what had caused her so much pain. She wondered where she had gone wrong. After working long hours and travelling all over the country, Caroline realised she needed a balance between her work and her personal life. She felt comfortable with her work but not with men. Finally, one day, she took the plunge. Now she is settled in a caring and loving relationship.

From my personal experience, after my marriage broke up, I know I felt worse than a teenager when I began dating again—if that's possible! My hands shook, my heart pounded and I couldn't wait until the experience was over. But I went back for more and my children were very supportive of me.

Many professional counsellors say it takes about five years to get over the trauma of a marriage break-up. Having been divorced for many years now I have enjoyed the time alone with my children. I have felt happy being independent and have shared an awful lot with my children. We have worked through all the emotional ups and downs, openly discussing how we felt, releasing anger, frustration, guilt, and grief when we needed to and our lives have followed the right path for us both as individuals and as a family.

Mix and match

When single parents get together for a day out it can be like an episode of 'The Brady Bunch' on vacation. But blended families can be stressful too. There are different aspects that may affect everyone if not dealt with carefully, and different backgrounds, upbringing, discipline, as well as mixing the sexes, possessiveness and jealousy, can be a volatile mix.

When introducing a new partner into your children's lives a slow and balanced approach is advisable. If you are seen spending more time with your new partner your children will get upset. If you spend too much time with your children your partner may decide to find someone else.

When the children meet one another there has to be a settling period, finding where each one stands, who has seniority, who can do what with whom, and how far boundaries can be stretched.

A trying time for the lovers to watch and, as long as it isn't destructive or resentful, this is a situation that must be sorted out by those who command it—the children!

Joined for a reason

Even after a family has been divided into two homes, family life can carry on because of the common factor—the children. It is wonderful if parents can stay friends, although many don't, but where possible it is important to work together on major decisions and important issues, supporting one another in essential discipline.

It is important for children to see unity—they should not hear criticism by one partner about the other. After all, your former partner is still their mother or father and needs their respect and love. Putting your former partner down in front of your children undermines the relationship.

What has happened in your relationship is between you and your partner, and your children can make up their own minds about it.

Coping skills

Positive sayings to help your children cope with what life brings

- I am coping with what life has put in my path.
- I am a wonderful human being who is doing all the right things at the right time.
- My life is in order and everything is happening as it is meant to.
- I am allowed to cry and feel my loss. The memories may fade but will never die.

Serenity bubbles

A meditation to help your children deal with loss and move on

Take life slowly, at your own pace. Do what you feel comfortable with because this is a very vulnerable time for you. Now lie down and gently close your eyes. I want you to take three deep breaths slowly. Feel the air filling your lungs and then being expelled. Your body feels heavier and heavier as you lie here gently breathing.

As you lie here quiet and still, a beautiful white light surrounds you like a great big bubble. You are wrapped up in a place that is safe and warm. The bubble is transparent and you can see everything outside. Everything outside your bubble seems a little fuzzy at first but as you focus you notice things becoming clearer. All the people you love are outside the bubble looking in. They know you are safe and warm in your bubble and they are happy for you. Sitting right beside you is a jar full of soapy water and a special stick that makes bubbles. I want you to pick the stick up, put it in the soapy water and blow a bubble. The bubble floats gently in the air. Rainbow colours stream through the bubble where the sunlight catches it. The bubble you have blown pops out through your bubble into the air outside and floats away. When you blow your next bubble think about all the things that are worrying you or making you feel sad. Put them in the bubble and watch as the bubble passes out away from you and then bursts, sending colour droplets of water into the air—gone. Fill the next bubble with all the things that are making you angry; put them in the bubble and send them on their way, never to be seen again, as again they burst into tiny little droplets.

When you blow the next bubble think about someone you wish to talk to, someone you want to say something to, whether it is a person or an animal that has left you or if it is someone still close to you. Put your thoughts into the bubble as you blow it. Watch as it gently floats away, completely whole. Trust that the person you are sending a message to can hear you. You can lie here and send as many bubbles as you want to as many people as you want. Take your time and think about what you are saying and release and let go of any bad or sad thoughts.

When you are ready open your eyes. You can come back to your safe bubble whenever you feel the need. This is a safe place, a place where you can cry and get rid of anything that makes you feel sad or angry.

Suggested Australian Bush Flower Essences

To cope with accidents and trauma: Boronia, Jacaranda, Sundew, Red Lily, Mountain Devil, Fringed Violet

To relieve anxiety: Dog Rose, Crowea

To restore balance: Jacaranda, Bush Fuchsia, Crowea

To relieve depression: Kapok Bush, Flannel Flower, Wild Potato Bush, Red Grevillea

To alleviate headaches: Emergency Essence, Five Corners, Paw Paw, Sturt Desert Rose

To cope with a nervous breakdown: Black-eyed Susan, Old Man Banksia, Fringed Violet, Jacaranda, Paw Paw

To help with shock: Emergency Essence, Fringed Violet
To deal with stomach problems: Paw Paw, Crowea, Dog Rose, Billy Goat Plum

Parents' page

Suggestions to help you and your children through a period of grief and guilt

1. Talk with your children as honestly as you can. They don't need to know all the ins and outs, but they do need to know how you feel just as much as you need to know how they are feeling.
2. Really listen to what your children have to say; their thoughts and feelings are important.
3. Let your children know that they will have good days and bad days. Tell them you are always there for them and your door is always open regardless of whether they think it is dumb, frightening, or scary. Keep your heart and mind open.
4. Reassure your children that life will go on regardless. Try to keep your normal activities up, although having some quality time for yourself is important too. Get in touch with your thoughts and feelings. Taking some personal time as a single parent is not easy when trying to fit in children, your job, housework, and so on, but a few minutes here and there are invaluable. In your quiet moments realise and acknowledge what you have achieved and if you have achieved goals on your own they should be a great boost to your morale and self-esteem.
5. Seek advice from a counsellor who reflects your thoughts, beliefs (and budget). It is great to be able to bounce your thoughts and feelings off a neutral person. Release all your positive and negative thoughts

and you will see how normal your reactions are. Find a counsellor for your children at school and make them aware of your children's situation. Give your children permission to talk to the counsellor at any time about anything they want to.

6. Talk with their teachers and make them aware of what is going on so they can be alert to unusual behaviour or sudden outbursts of crying and sadness. Sometimes all your children need is a cuddle and a few kind words to help them move on to the next minute of their precious lives. If the pressure is too much their teachers will be able to help alleviate it.
7. Give your children another adult's telephone number as a contact in case they need someone to talk to.
8. Tell your children that the break-up or loss is not their fault. It is between you and your partner and they are not to blame.
9. Watch the family's diet—it is very easy to eat too much or too little at these times. If a big meal is too much for your children to face then little snacks are great, but keep all your energies up so that tiredness and frayed nerves are kept at bay.
10. Changing clubs or changing routines can help start a new life. For instance, we changed swimming venues and clubs, the children were put into one school instead of two, we moved address and we worked out new ways of doing things that suited us as a family. A new beginning is important, it leaves the past not forgotten but a memory.
11. Teach your family relaxation techniques that address the stress you are experiencing. Using meditation separately or together is great for bonding, and is a non-judgemental way of getting in touch with your thoughts, feelings and emotions, and then releasing them in a positive way.
12. Gradually introduce your children to the idea that you

will venture out into the adult world of relationships one day. Again talk about what is going on in your life, reassuring your children that no one will ever replace the person you have lost, but that you do deserve love in your life and someone to share it with.

13. Reassure your children you will also always be there for them whenever they need you even if there is someone else in your life.
14. Your children don't have to like your new partner or your partner's children, although that would be ideal, but a healthy respect between all family members is important to dissipate any jealousy or hate that arises.
15. When other children are involved it is sometimes best to let them sort out their own places in the combined family, as long as no one is being put down, teased, degraded or hurt.
16. Let your children and other members of your new family know how wonderful, special and unique they all are. Each one of you has a special role to play and you can help each other grow and expand as individuals.

All of the therapies outlined in this book are excellent for helping you and your family get through this period. All of them can be used to help release feelings of guilt and grief and allow you to move on.

The right path for me—positive sayings to help build healthy family relationships

- I am a wonderful parent who is bringing up my children to the very best of my ability.
- My life is on the right path. I am fulfilling my life's purpose now and always.
- I draw the people and the situations I need for me to make my life calm and relaxed, successful and productive.

- My family and I are working together in perfect harmony. We are one.

Touching lives—a meditation to help you cope with guilt and grief

Take this time to grieve and start to heal yourself. If you find you want to cry, allow the tears to flow and acknowledge your feelings. If you experience anger, let it flow—go along with whatever you feel. Lie or sit down and get really comfortable. Now close your eyes. I want you to take three deep, long, slow breaths. As you take each breath in, imagine a beautiful white light. As you breathe out, let go of any negative thoughts. The white light fills your body, mind and soul. Its energy engulfs your whole being. You are at peace. You are connected with your higher self. You are one. Spend just a moment in this space.

As you lie or sit here a gentle soul comes to your side. You feel their spirit, and realise you know this person. Whether you have lost this person through death, separation or divorce they are here with you now in spirit. As they stand by your side you touch their hand and you feel the energy flow freely between you. This lifts both of your spirits to a higher awareness.

You are aware of the very core of this being, the energy, the spirit, and it is full of love. The connection between the two of you, whether good or bad in the past, is now lost in the universal power. You have been a part of one another's lives for a reason. Take the opportunity to thank that person for what they have shared with you. You may want to forgive them for something they have done, or perhaps there was so much more you wanted to say when they were here, or you just want to thank them. Take your time—there is no need to hurry.

If you wish to cry, acknowledge it. If you want to say something out loud speak freely and truly from the heart.

Acknowledge, release and let go of your thoughts, feelings and emotions. This is your time—take it.

When you are ready, say goodbye and let go of the other soul. Remember, you can call on them again if you have more to say or share. Now as you turn to go, place your feet firmly on the ground and ask to be placed in the right direction for your highest purpose. You see yourself on your path at peace and in harmony with the universe. You are heading towards your dreams and goals—all you have to do is ask and you will receive help.

When you feel you have completed what you set out to do open your eyes. When you awake you will be able to express yourself in a way that is cleansing and purifying to your soul.

Suggested Australian Bush Flower Essences

To cope with accidents and trauma: Boronia, Jacaranda, Sundew, Red Lily, Mountain Devil, Fringed Violet
To relieve anxiety: Dog Rose, Crowea
To restore balance: Jacaranda, Bush Fuchsia, Crowea
To cope with depression: Kapok Bush, Flannel Flower, Wild Potato Bush, Red Grevillea
To alleviate headaches: Emergency Essence, Five Corners, Paw Paw, Sturt Desert Rose
To cope with a nervous breakdown: Black-eyed Susan, Old Man Banksia, Fringed Violet, Jacaranda, Paw Paw
To deal with shock: Emergency Essence, Fringed Violet
To alleviate stomach problems: Paw Paw, Crowea, Dog Rose, Billy Goat Plum

The final chapter of Part One is about how to face and deal with the challenges in life that you and your family may encounter. Part Two explores seven alternative therapies you may like to introduce to your family life to help you all heal from the various situations and emotions that may befall you.

14
DEPRESSION

Every cloud has a silver lining.

In the last few chapters we have discussed many of the crises and emotions that you and your family may experience as you face the challenges of life. In this chapter we are going to learn about depression. According to health statistics, mental health problems and disorders affect one in five children; these include depression, anxiety, Attention Deficit Disorder (ADD), grief, eating disorders and suicide. The figures are staggering, as approximately two-fifths of young people suffer from depressed moods in any six-month period and 50 per cent of teenagers who suffer a depressive incident may have one or more recurrence of a depressive disorder later on. Approximately one-third of young people diagnosed with a depressive disorder will attempt suicide within twenty years.

All children feel sad sometimes but when sadness is experienced for a long period of time, like over a few weeks, professional help may be needed to help your children get over what is troubling them, as sadness can turn into depression. Many children, especially teenagers, experience mood swings due to hormone changes in their bodies. They are experiencing changes mentally, physically and socially, and many find it difficult to express their feelings and may even deny that anything is wrong. When children experience depression their denial changes the way they act and react and their behaviour may appear out of character. They may become aggressive or belligerent, and may take part in risky behaviour, for example, turning to drugs or alcohol, compounding their problems.

Depression is usually caused by external stressors, such as:

- separation
- divorce
- death of a close family member or pet
- arrival of a new family member
- illness or perceived illness
- loss of home or security
- abuse (physical, mental or emotional)
- unemployment
- learning difficulties
- victimisation
- poor relationships
- a crisis in sexual identity
- drugs and alcohol.

Depression can also be genetic, passed on by a biological relative, or caused by a body chemical imbalance.

Depression needs to be taken very seriously by every parent and needs early intervention and treatment. If you detect any of the following telltale signs or suspect your children are suffering from depression, find someone your children can trust and talk to, for example a counsellor, a doctor or a close friend. It is important to set up a support network for your children. Your children's support network may or may not include the family network depending on the circumstances, but this needs to be discussed with your children.

It is important to get children who are suffering from depression to make decisions on how to go about their treatment and recovery. This helps them re-build their self-esteem and confidence, and gives them a sense of responsibility, helping them to feel capable and useful. Once a network has been set up to help sufferers deal with their problems, it is essential that all matters discussed are kept confidential, unless they are at risk of harming themselves or others.

How can we tell whether our children are just sad or are suffering from depression? Here are some telltale signs of depression in children:

- They seem very sad and irritable.
- They cry more frequently or feel guilty about family problems.
- They gain or lose weight suddenly.
- They seem fearful or restless.
- They either run away from school or don't want to go to school.
- They lack concentration or have poor performance in school work.
- Their sleeping habits change.
- They blame themselves for everything that goes wrong.
- They become aggressive or hostile.
- They lack motivation, enthusiasm and energy.
- They feel useless, worthless, hopeless and have poor self-esteem.
- They don't take part in the activities they usually enjoy.
- They get involved in risk-taking behaviour.
- They seem antisocial, and isolate themselves from others.
- They are impulsive.
- They talk about death and suicide.

Sadness and depression can be dealt with positively and effectively if recognised early on. We need to educate our children about depression so that they don't feel the need to turn to risk-taking behaviour such as experimenting with drugs and alcohol.

I really feel for Trudi, a woman who agreed to be interviewed for this book, as all she has left of her teenage son is a photograph and her memories. Adam suffered from depression for a few years after his parents, Trudi and Chris, divorced. His parents were aware of his mood swings but put them down to just being a teenager.

Adam loved music and his dream in life was to be a musician. But his dream faded as he became more and more depressed. He seemed to have lost interest in everything. He got involved with the wrong sort of people and started taking drugs and drinking alcohol, which simply made matters worse. He started stealing, even from his parents, to pay for his addictions.

Finally, after several family discussions, Adam agreed to seek medical help but he couldn't cope with the idea of going through with it. A month later he committed suicide. Trudi and Chris were devastated. Both of them suffered from guilt. Had they done everything they could? Could they have prevented such a devastating outcome? Both parents had to go for counselling to help them deal with their guilt, grief and loss. Trudi says the guilt still haunts her today.

Drugs and alcohol

Experimenting with drugs and alcohol is the sort of risk-taking behaviour your children may adopt to help them deal with depression. Unfortunately many children and teenagers believe that these mind-altering substances will help alleviate their feelings when in fact they only make things worse.

Drugs and alcohol may suppress their true feelings for a time, but soon the mood-altering substances don't have the same effect, leading to increased use and dependency. If you discover that your children have turned to either drugs or alcohol, help and support them in finding ways to free themselves from their addictions. Show them they are worthy of a good life.

Balanced

Positive sayings for your children to help them keep their life on track

- I am a worthy person who deserves love now and always.
- I am a beautiful person who deserves the very best of everything.
- I am able to solve my problems quickly and effectively.
- I am free of any addictions that stop me from being the real me.
- I am able to cope with everything life presents to me, without taking any form of mood-altering substance.
- I think and act clearly because my body is free from alcohol and drugs.
- I have people around me that are there for my highest good.

Fly with the eagles

A meditation to help your children to attract the right situations and people and to express themselves with honesty and openness

Lie down and get really comfortable. Imagine a beautiful golden light streaming down on your head and going down your body to your arms, filling every part of you. You can feel and see the light flow down you, all the way down to the end of each of your toes. Lie here absorbing the golden light as it calms and heals you. Now imagine the golden light turning green. You feel the sensation as the green light swirls around your body and accept the love that it gives you.

Now imagine you are climbing up the side of a hill. You place your feet firmly on the ground. With each step you take you become stronger and stronger. You feel the wind brush your face. Imagine it blowing away all bad or negative thoughts. Allow all these thoughts to be taken far away. You have now reached the top of the mountain. Look out across the land. Notice how you feel. A golden eagle circles in the blue sky above you. How regal and mighty it looks. Imagine yourself flying with the eagle. You soar in the wind. A wave of silence, peace, harmony and calm flows through you. You are like the eagle when you experience highs and lows in your life. You need to face your fears, broaden your outlook and give yourself permission to achieve your heart's desire. You are always able to express what you feel with clarity and meaning. You speak from your heart and you always say and do the right thing because you are a good communicator.

Now you have the people in your life who can help you to grow. You are a unique human being; an individual who has purpose and meaning. Now you are able to move on with your life and deal with any new challenges. You draw only good situations and people to you. You know you deserve only the very best in life and the energy of life flows through you at all times. Even when you are feeling lost you will be able to find your way home because you have the strength and the power of an eagle. As you glide on a stream of warm air take a moment to listen for any messages that the eagle has to share with you. When you are ready open your eyes and bring yourself back into the here and now.

Parents' page

A parent's instincts are very strong—you know when something isn't right. Go with your gut feelings. Keep in touch with your children whatever age they are. Communicate with them. Talk. Let them know they can come to you any time, night or day, regardless of what has happened or what might happen. Get to know their friends, who they are with, what they do, where they go.

Sometimes parents can see that something isn't quite right with their children but they are too embarrassed or too proud to ask for help. Early detection of depression in your children is essential for the best possible outcome. If you are not sure whether your children are depressed ask your doctor, a paediatrician, or your children's school teachers for their opinion. Ask them if they think your children's behaviour is normal. Then find out who can help you and your family with this challenge. You will need people to help you and your children develop social skills to cope with life in a positive way, emotionally, physically and mentally, so your children can rebuild their self-esteem and self-confidence. Your children may also need help to reconstruct and enhance friendships and relationships that are floundering. Counsellors and other health professionals help with your children's attitudes and behaviour, encouraging them to fit back into society without stigma and fear. Through an appropriate assessment, a health professional will determine the correct treatment for an individual and for your family, as well as helping you to build a support network.

Things we can do as parents and as a family to help

There are many things we can do as parents and as a family to help when our children show signs of depression. We can start by seeking professional help but it is also important to back this up with family support. For instance, we can:

- take time to do things with our children that they enjoy.
- encourage them to spend time with friends.
- encourage them to exercise, take up a sport, or indulge in their favourite hobbies.
- keep them focused on positive activities .
- get them involved in self-development programmes or groups.
- get them to talk to someone they trust.

- encourage them to ask for help whenever it is needed.
- take care to be sincere in all we say and do, so that they feel they are really loved and cared for.
- be there for them and stay loving, caring and supportive of them no matter what.

As I outlined in the chapter on stress, if one family member is stressed the rest of the family will be too. You need to keep a positive outlook, taking each day as it comes. Blaming yourself or others for what is happening is destructive and negative, so come together and work on the solution for a successful outcome. Everyone in the family will be experiencing emotions and feelings such as guilt, blame, grief, shame, anger, denial, rejection, disorientation and even depression to some degree, so it is important to look after yourself and your family. Do things for yourself to help you cope. You may want to begin by finding a counsellor to help deal with your emotions. Some people prefer to relate to other people in similar situations or support groups for people who are going through the same thing as you. Allow yourself to feel and express your emotions. If you feel like crying—cry. It is a great healer. Try to turn this experience into a positive. Ask yourself how this experience can improve your way of living in the future. Meditate and pray to the God of your understanding for guidance and help, and ask for help when you need it.

All the therapies I have outlined in this book are of benefit for overcoming depression, but discuss them with your health professional, a doctor or counsellor, first to make sure you are not undoing any of their work. Many therapists recommend meditation and prayer to help your children become calm and relaxed even in times of trauma and crisis. You may choose to encourage your children to have a massage and a bubble bath to relax and release tension. Help them to acknowledge their feelings by getting them to write them down in a journal or draw them. Most of all love them—show them they are very special human beings with a lot to offer the world. Finally, if your children should talk about death or suicide, get medical help immediately. Children do not talk about these things lightly.

I have included two meditations in this section, one for love and forgiveness, and the other for strength, direction and courage.

Supporting mechanisms—positive sayings to help you cope when your children are depressed

- I am aware of everything around me and can deal with all situations in a positive way which leads to a positive outcome.
- I know that everything happens for a reason and I am able to cope with what life puts before me.
- I release and let go of any anxiety about my children. I trust my children.
- What my children do is their responsibility. I guide them along the right path at all times.
- I allow myself to release and let go of any pain and anger in a positive manner and am healing my heart, mind, body and soul.
- I take each day as it comes, with a positive outlook. I am able to get in touch with myself, express my emotions and move on.
- I can deal with whatever life has to offer me no matter how hard it seems.

Love and forgiveness—a meditation to help you cope with depression in your family

Take three deep, slow breaths. As you breathe in imagine all the goodness of the universe filling your soul. As you breathe out imagine all negative thoughts and feelings flowing out of every cell in your body. Release and let go. Now imagine a white light coming down through the top of your head.

Imagine this light flows down your neck, across your shoulders, your arms, down through your body, down your legs to the end of your toes. You lie in the white light and absorb every ray as they shine gloriously through you. This light passes through your skin out into your aura. You feel it clearing and healing you as it shines brighter and brighter.

Now imagine you are lying on a beautiful sandy beach. The sun is high in the sky and warms your body. The sea splashes your feet, as waves gently lap across the sand. Feel the sand through your fingers. It is warm. As you lie here someone comes to sit by your side. You are really pleased to see them. You take their hand and together you walk along the beach.

As you walk with this person, you hear the word 'forgiveness' and feel compassion pouring through your heart, mind, body and soul. Embrace the words 'forgiveness' or 'forgive' with all your heart. As you go on further you hear the word 'blameless' and feel its grace and purity pour through your heart, mind, body and soul. Embrace the word 'blameless' with all your heart. Now with each step you take you are becoming stronger and each step is the right step in the right direction. Further on you hear the word 'serenity' and feel its tranquillity in your heart, mind, body and soul. Embrace the word 'serenity' with all your heart. Finally you come to the end of the beach and face your friend. You hear the word 'love' and feel love pouring through your heart, mind, body and soul. Embrace the word 'love' with all your heart. Now release any thoughts, feelings and emotions and let go. You are safe.

When you are ready return to the here and now. Understand that you are getting stronger day by day.

Time out—a meditation to build your strength and courage and help you find a new direction

Lie down and get really comfortable. Gently close your eyes. As you lie here quiet and still take three deep breaths. As you breathe in imagine a beautiful white light filling your heart, mind and soul. When you breathe out let go of anything worrying or painful. You take three long, deep, strong breaths and the white light fills your whole being; mind, body and spirit. Relax in the white light and enjoy the sensation it gives you.

Imagine you are lying on a bed in a large room. Look around and observe the decor. It may be old-fashioned or modern. Take in every detail. Notice smells wafting around you. Incense is burning somewhere nearby. A young person enters the room carrying a big old-fashioned reed fan. They start to fan you gently and you feel the air gently caress your skin. Gather all your negative thoughts and feelings and let them drift away with the air that is fanning you. Let all your anger and frustration dissipate in the breeze. Another person comes to your side. They have brought oils to massage your feet and hands. Feel that soothing touch as they massage you slowly and with expert attention—absorb the love, care and attention being given to you. You are love.

Another person comes to you with a bowl of your favourite food. They feed you by hand—you have nothing to do but eat the food until you feel totally satisfied. Know now you can tackle any situation that is given to you. You feel extremely relaxed, calm and pampered to the fullest and your senses are keen and alert.

A child comes to you and you realise it is your child who is experiencing difficulties with an addiction. As they stand before you let them know you forgive them for everything. Let them know you are there to support them whatever they do. Tell them you love them no matter what they do or say. This child appears to be bound by their own limitations. Ask how you can help them and listen to what they say. Ask your child if they would like to be fanned, massaged and fed and invite them to lie on the bed next to you. If the child refuses don't worry, let them go. If they decide they want to be pampered with the luxuries of life then let them lie next to you and enjoy the attention. When you have finished talking and being pampered, open your eyes and know that you are relaxed and have a new direction and more confidence to deal with what is happening to you and your child.

Suggested Australian Bush Flower Essences

For unnerving situations or emotions: Emergency Essence
To relieve anxiety: Dog Rose, Crowea
To restore balance: Jacaranda, Bush Fuchsia, Crowea
To cope with depression: Kapok Bush, Flannel Flower, Wild Potato Bush, Red Grevillea
To aid forgiveness: Dagger Hakea
To release frustration: Old Man Banksia, Black-eyed Susan, Jacaranda, Sunshine Wattle, Red Grevillea

In Part Two I describe seven alternative therapies that I have personally chosen to use with my children and found interesting and successful. On your life's journey you will discover many other therapies. Some you may want to try straight away and others you may not be sure about. If you investigate and research new therapies, applying what you learn in Part Two, you will know if they are suitable for you and your family.

Part Two

Alternative Therapies: the Tools of Intuitive Parenting

INTRODUCTION

In the next few chapters we will explore some alternative therapies that you may like to introduce to your family. Although many alternative therapies may seem like new ideas, often they are ancient remedies that have been used for thousands of years, and we are only now realising the difference they can make to our lives. Alternative therapies help us get in touch with the real cause of illness instead of just looking at the physical ailment or outcome. They help us to balance our mental, physical and spiritual sides. When we suppress our emotions we become depressed, suffer from poor self-image and self-worth, and our performance is poor, but if we learn to acknowledge our needs and desires, releasing and letting go of our emotions, we can lead healthier, more successful lives. As parents, we need to be in touch with who we are and so do our children.

Today many doctors and psychologists recommend the use of alternative therapies such as acupuncture, journalling, dream therapy and meditation to complement conventional medicine. Some forms of therapeutic massage are widely used in conventional medicine. Most health insurance funds now offer levels of cover which include a range of alternative treatments and a growing number of family medical centres have alternative and natural therapists available for consultation. If you choose to explore alternative therapies, please note it is recommended that these complement conventional medicine and in many circumstances a medical consultation is necessary for diagnosis and treatment of a condition, especially if symptoms persist. Alternative therapies do not claim to cure illness or disease and you are advised to inform your doctor if you undertake a course of therapy.

Let us begin our journey into alternative therapies. The seven therapies we will explore are:

1. Affirmations
2. Aromatherapy
3. Australian Bush Flower Essences
4. Journalling
5. Kinergetics
6. Massage
7. Meditation

Following these chapters is a resources chapter for your reference with contact details which may be of use to you and your family.

1

AFFIRMATIONS AND PRAYER

When we devote our mind, body and soul to a belief in a power higher than ourselves, all we dream and hope for will become reality.

Affirm on the wings of a prayer

Affirmations and prayer have played a big part in my life. I first learnt about positive affirmations many years ago when I picked up a book called *The Power of Positive Thinking* by Dr. Norman Vincent Peale. After reading his book and trying to implement many things Dr. Peale wrote about, I had the great pleasure of hearing him speak when I was attending a Professional Speakers Convention in America. It was a great thrill indeed because his work inspired me so much, making me realise that I could achieve my goals and my dreams and make a success of my life at a time when I was questioning what life was all about.

Dr. Peale maintains that what you put in your brain is what you get out of it. The brain cannot differentiate between good, bad, right or wrong, so the more positive information you feed it, the better your self talk will be. When we are positive we keep focused on where we are heading in our lives. When life is not going as we want, we have to find ways to turn our situation into positive actions and reactions. When we have a positive attitude towards life we feel good about ourselves and have more confidence. When there is an internal conflict between our personality and our attitudes we become anxious, stressed, frustrated and we lack self-worth and confidence. One way to build ourselves up again is to use positive affirmations. An affirmation is a positive statement about our being and our lives. Affirmation means to validate and make firm.

The daily use of positive affirmations and prayer gives our souls a belief in the here and now as well as the future.

Creating affirmations for your family

Introducing positive affirmations to your family will change the way you all act and think. It builds a positive way of thinking which builds healthy attitudes that breed success. It also builds healthy relationships. Are you aware that for every negative thought, ten positive thoughts are needed to counter the negativity? So start teaching your family to use affirmations.

How we form and implement these statements is very important. When you write an affirmation always make the statement positive and personal. The statement must begin with 'I' and be written in words that you use. It should also be in the present tense rather than the past or the future. For example, 'I am', not 'I will', or 'I am going to'. Your affirmation should be powerful. The power of the statement depends on the ability of the individual and must suit them at this moment. For instance, young children must make the statement according to their own ability. The statement needs to be short so it can be easily remembered, and be specific. And be careful what you ask for because you might get it!

Children are very good at making statements about themselves, so the above guidelines are important to help them work for the best possible outcome. Help your children form their affirmations and then help them use them in their daily lives. Writing them down or saying them once won't make them a reality. Affirmations need to be looked at on a daily basis and affirmed over and over again. The following ideas may help you and your children to use your affirmations effectively and make your dreams come true.

1. Write the affirmations down 10 times every day, preferably in a journal.
2. Spend time putting the affirmations together in a creative way. Make it fun.
3. Put the affirmations where they can be seen, for example on the fridge, in a wallet, by the bed, on the bedroom door.
4. Read them out loud each day with real feeling and believe they are becoming reality.

Affirmations are very powerful and can be used along with the other therapies mentioned in Part Two. As your children work more and more with positive affirmations they will come to realise they can take responsibility for creating their own lives. They will understand that what they put into their heads has the possibility of becoming their reality. They will find that their lives become more manageable and successful through positive thoughts. Here are some examples of affirmations:

- I am giving and receiving unconditional love now and always.
- I deserve the very best life has to offer me.
- I am a beautiful person.
- Nature's light shines through me.
- I am successful in everything I set out to do.
- I am good at my school work and I make like-minded friends easily.

On the wings of a prayer

Prayer is very private. It links us with a higher source. It is a very personal connection which should be revered and undertaken whenever you or your children feel the need. As parents we are responsible for the guidance of our children in their mental, physical and spiritual directions. Prayer needs to be taught so that it is effective and comes straight from the heart. We usually pray when we desire or seek guidance, help, or forgiveness, or when we just want to give thanks. It is a time to trust that all our prayers will be answered.

I have prayed since I was a little girl. There have been times when I have strayed from my beliefs, have doubted a higher power, or have just not bothered to find the time to pray. But my daily prayers have proven to me that prayer is a very powerful tool for making miracles happen.

I was taught to pray at an early age. As a Sunday School teacher, I taught many young children to pray, but my whole approach to prayer changed when I was introduced to a wonderful book called *The Science of the Mind* by Ernest Holmes. Holmes believed in a power greater than ourselves that we could call upon to help us create our reality. I continued to research the power of prayer and learnt that while people pray in different places and at different times, everyone who prays hopes for a connection that will lift their spirits. Some people prefer not to pray to God but pray to a higher power: a God of their own personal understanding.

As with affirmations, it is very important to be specific about what you ask for in prayer because you may get precisely what you asked for which may not be what you had in mind. We may not get everything we ask for immediately because we are not ready yet. Be patient and be prepared to ask for guidance and listen to what you are being told. Wait for the answers to your prayers to be revealed to you. Have faith. Sometimes I keep asking for a particular outcome and

I feel as if my prayers are in vain. When I stop to look the answer is there and has been all the time. I just hadn't seen it.

Experience prayer with your children—link your souls and become one in this beautiful universe of ours. You may like to share the following framework for prayer with your children. I have found it highly effective. Please adapt the word 'God' to your own beliefs. Begin by acknowledging that God is everything and everywhere and you are a part of God. Talk to God and ask for guidance. If you want something to happen or you want a certain outcome know that God has your best interests at heart. As you ask know that you deserve the best life has to offer. Give thanks to God for all life holds for you and be thankful for what life gives you. Acknowledge and have faith that what you have asked for will be presented to you. Then release and let go of your prayer and trust that it is becoming reality now. Believe your prayers are being answered now. When you ask questions be prepared for the answers; listen and look for signs. Be ready—the God of your understanding moves in mysterious ways.

Forgiveness

Sometimes when we have difficulties in a relationship we need to look at the core issues. Quite often we blame others rather than looking within ourselves to find out what part we played in the breakdown of a relationship. Often both parties are at fault. We can use prayer to ask for forgiveness for ourselves and others.

A friend of mine, Peter, had a spat with his colleague, Simon, at work and they didn't talk to each other for several days. Peter was quite within his right to say what he did but perhaps the way he had said it could have been better.

For a few days Peter asked through prayer to be given guidance on how to deal with the situation which was very tense and uncomfortable for both him and Simon. He also asked for forgiveness for Simon because Peter felt he was in the right. Peter prayed for several days until, finally, he and Simon had to face one another and speak.

Although both Peter and Simon were angry and hurt, their differences were diffused by a higher power, as they were placed in a situation where they were able to talk amicably, as if nothing had happened.

If you know that you have done something wrong ask for forgiveness and make amends in your prayer, something or someone will appear to help you get over the situation and emotions you are feeling. The incident will pass. As I said at the beginning of the chapter, what we think becomes our reality.

A prayer for forgiveness of the self

This is a guided prayer to forgive yourself for any thought, action or reaction that you may wish forgiveness for. If you wish to forgive another person for their wrongdoing you can adapt this prayer, asking for the other person to be forgiven, acknowledging that they are sick and need help from a power greater than yourself. Ask that they will receive healing and help that is for their highest good. If you are needed to help this person, ask for knowledge of how to go about it. Follow what your heart tells you.

> To the God of my understanding
>
> Almighty God, God of infinite power, wisdom, love and understanding. God of all the universe, nature and beauty. God of forgiveness. I acknowledge you here and now as an essence in all things including my heart, body and soul. We are as one.
>
> Dear Lord, I ask forgiveness for my thoughts, actions and deeds, and ask that you show me how I can be of better service to you in

all I do. I ask that you show me truth so that I may live my life according to your will, not that of my own or of others.

I know the correct path for me to walk is being revealed to me now. I am aware of your love, support and guidance, and I am achieving the very best from this situation.

Dear Lord, I feel your courage and strength fill my heart, body and soul. I know you are always by my side when I need clarity and purpose in my thoughts and deeds.

I thank you for hearing my prayer. I feel your forgiveness flow over me, washing my self-centred attitudes away. Thank you for all the miracles that are happening to me every day. I now release my prayer knowing you have forgiven me for what I have done. I understand that my life has a clear direction again so that I may fulfil my highest purpose.

I have heard many stories about people who have found the answers to their lives in prayer. Many of them aren't religious and often they don't know who they are praying to. They just know it works.

One story I came across was from a young man who had a drug problem. After he had been in a detoxification centre, he joined a group made of people who had been in a similar position. They shared their stories and experiences which helped each person recover from drug abuse. This group believed prayer worked and so the young man put his faith in praying daily to a higher power of his understanding. As weeks went on his life came together. Every day he noticed that the things he asked for in his prayer happened or he was led to people or places where his prayers were answered. His prayers were not always answered the way he wanted but he soon realised that, when they didn't, the outcome was for his highest good anyway.

This young man found a strength in his faith he had never

known before. He thanked his God for all the good things in life, asked for guidance and help when needed and believed that whatever happened his higher power would see him through, no matter how challenging his life became. He understood that his God is a God of love and He only wants the best for him.

2
AROMATHERAPY

The whiff of a certain aroma can send us reeling into raptures of ecstasy.

The essential oil

In Part One we identified some difficult situations and crises we may encounter as parents. Now we are exploring the tools we can use in our everyday lives to help create calmer, more successful, fulfilled children. Aromatherapy is a unique tool for altering our moods and affecting our environment at home, at work or at play.

Everything in and around us that is connected to nature has a way of giving us answers to our questions. We have become so sophisticated as a society, with our advances in the fields of technology, medicine, and our exploration of the universe, but we very rarely use our five senses to the fullest. We rely on our sight, hearing, sense of smell, taste and touch but how often do we develop and enhance these senses to our advantage? How often do we rely on outside influences to make our decisions for us? Life is moving so fast, we grab what we can, when we can, in order to get the instant gratification we desire. We crave the simple life and the old, tried and true remedies, which rely on the use of intuition and the five senses.

Aromatherapy is an ancient healing art that was practised by the Hebrews, Greeks, Egyptians and Chinese thousands of years ago, using essential oils that have been extracted from flowers, trees, bushes, herbs, stems, roots and barks for healing qualities. Now aromatherapy is being used in hospitals, medical clinics and some children's centres. One detoxification clinic I know encourages patients to use lavender oil in their baths and on their person to help them remain calm as they detoxify. Aromatherapy is a natural form of healing that is gentle, pleasant and acts through the sense of smell. I find this therapy very soothing and sensual and really enjoy shopping for the oils, and testing the different fragrances and perfumes.

As you know we all react differently to different scents and our sense of smell is reputed to be the strongest sense memory. The smell of burning toast reminds me of my mother's kitchen! Walking past a window of a kitchen where freshly baked biscuits have just come out of the oven sends me into a homely, loving frame of mind. Their aroma entices me to eat even though I may not be hungry. A beautiful perfume will turn anyone's head and always gets an interesting response. The smell of smoke instinctively induces fear. A garden full of blossoms arouses all the senses, enhancing sensuality, awareness and temperament.

Recently I bought a jasmine bush because its perfume brings back memories of a house I lived in of which I have many fond memories. Now I live in a highly populated city suburb but my garden is full of lavender bushes with their beautiful, peaceful, calming aroma.

Buying and storing oils

The process of extracting the oils is difficult and time-consuming, and while some of the purest products are the most expensive they are often the most beneficial. As with most products on the market today there are cheaper oils but some of these are not as effective as using the purest oils and may end up costing you more in the long run. When you store your essential oils make sure you put them in a cool, dark place as they evaporate easily. And keep them stored securely away from your little children as many essential oils are poisonous and must never be taken internally. Never use essential oils directly on the skin without first blending and diluting them with a carrier oil.

Aromatherapy and your children

There are many ways you can introduce your children to aromatherapy. I introduced my children to the various oils and fragrances by taking them into an aromatherapy shop where we took the time to test each blended oil, discussing how and what we felt as we tried each one. Since then we have tried various products incorporating aromatherapy oils, for example bath bombs, bath capsules, candles and so on. Little girls seem to enjoy getting these things as birthday gifts from friends as they enjoy discussing how these products make them feel emotionally and physically.

How does aromatherapy work?

The essential oils are administered either through vaporisation or inhalation, bathing, compresses, or blended and diluted in a carrier oil. Some may be used directly on the skin, or in massage. A chemical reaction occurs when the oil is inhaled, and enters the bloodstream via capillaries in the nose, throat and lungs. This creates either a calming or stimulating effect on the body depending on which essential oil is used. A psychological response also occurs as the olfactory centre in the brain is stimulated when the fragrance is inhaled. This in turn affects mood and hormonal secretions. Aromatherapy is a highly successful holistic treatment and can be used with babies, small and big children. Treatment of children requires smaller dosages than adults. Experts recommend that adults who have normal skin should use no more than five drops of essential oil to each 10 ml of carrier oil; for children, no more than one or two drops per 10 ml of carrier oil. It is also suggested that if you are using a strong, stimulating oil you should use less than the recommended dose.

If you intend to use an oil directly on the skin, test it on a small area first in case the skin is sensitive or the person is allergic to the oil's properties. If there has been no adverse reaction after 24 hours, you can use the recommended dosage. When making up your oils, use no more than five essential oils in one mixture otherwise the healing will be less effective. Finally, mix only the quantities you need for maximum results. If you use too much it can have the reverse effect.

Choosing which oil or fragrance to use can be confusing, so try to work with your intuition. Children seem to know instinctively which fragrance they need. Encourage them to go with their gut instincts as with other areas of their lives. This intuitive selection helps them to get to know their bodies and needs which encourages them to take responsibility for their mental, spiritual and physical wellbeing. As they use different oils and fragrances you may discover that a lot of suppressed feelings and emotions are uncovered so be prepared to be supportive and a good listener.

There are many ways you can administer aromatherapy healing to your children and other members of your family. Be very careful with dosages and please note that if your children suffer from asthma, hay fever or any skin allergies ask the advice of an aromatherapist and check with your doctor before using essential oils in any way. If you are pregnant avoid using the following essential oils: Basil, Clary Sage, Cypress, Fennel, Ginger, Lemongrass, Marjoram, Peppermint, Thyme, Rose,

Rosemary and Sage. Judith White in *Aromatherapy, Blends for Life* recommends that no oils be used on the body for the first 16 weeks of pregnancy and only one aromatherapy bath per week after that.

Air sprays and vaporising

Children love the smell of essential oils burning and usually sense them straight away. There are many beautiful ceramic burners available but I believe that the electric burners are safer when you have children around, especially as you can leave them on for 24 hours a day. An advantage of leaving an electrical burner on is that it creates a certain mood within the children's bedroom and environment, and acts as a preventative medicinal aid, fighting off germs. It also helps to get rid of those dead sock smells and those under-the-bed smells.

Whichever burner you choose fill the top part of it with water and add 6–8 drops of essential oil. Very soon the aroma will fill the air, changing the energy of the room. We often use our burner in the bathroom when having a long, warm, relaxing bubble bath. The candle burner adds a certain ambience that helps us to relax even further especially after a hard day at work, school or on the sports field. We all sleep much better and deeper when we have relaxed in this way.

I know one husband who sometimes creates a relaxing mood for his wife to come home to after a long day at work. He lights little aromatic candles all over the house, plays soft relaxing music and fills the bath with warm water and lavender bath salts. Then he lights a burner with Ylang Ylang. The mood is set. What a way to spoil the one you love!

Instead of vaporising the essential oils you can make up a spray using a glass or stainless steel receptacle. Fill it with distilled or purified water and add 3–4 drops of essential oil to freshen a room or your car.

Bathing

Having a warm bath helps release muscle aches and pains but adding a few drops of an essential oil in your children's bath will also help relieve stress, tiredness, insomnia and aches, which is great after a morning of sport or a hard day at school. You can also use drops to revitalise your children if they feel sluggish. If your young children throw tantrums pop them in a warm bath with three drops of rosemary oil to help calm them down. One drop each of lavender, sage and geranium is extremely good for the girls of the family suffering from period pains. Teenagers who suffer from acne may like to put two drops of lavender, juniper and cajuput into their bath to help cleanse and clear the skin.

Massage oils

Massage and essential oils are magic. We all love being massaged and babies and children are no different. As you experiment with the oils and massage techniques, your children will learn to massage their own bodies, feet and hands, getting in touch with themselves and their feelings. See the chapter on massage for techniques to try. Massage relaxes your children and yourself, so it works both ways. Massaging with essential oils blended and diluted in a carrier oil or massage oil relieves stress, tension, pent-up emotions, muscle aches and pains, as well as improving blood circulation and stimulation of the skin. Children who suffer from sleepwalking can benefit from a massage with a carrier oil containing lavender oil as it helps them into a relaxed deep sleep. Young babies suffering from colic really benefit from a light massage of their abdomen with two drops of fennel oil mixed with half a teaspoon of a carrier or massage oil. Remember, essential oils must be diluted before putting them directly on the skin and never put an essential oil directly onto the skin unless it is recommended by your aromatherapist and you have consulted with your doctor. And always keep them away from the eyes and mouth.

Just a drop on the pillow, sleeve, handkerchief . . .

A couple of drops of the diluted blended oil in any of these places can be very effective. I pop a couple of drops of lavender on my children's pillow at night to help calm and relax them. I remember my grandmother keeping lavender sachets in her handkerchief drawer so that each time she used a fresh handkerchief she was able to smell the calm, relaxing scent. In times of stress I put a couple of drops of blended lavender oil on my wrists, sleeve, or temples to help me relax. The scents children seem to enjoy the most are tangerine, orange, benzoin, cinnamon, spearmint and lime. Other essential oils that are beneficial for your family include:

Basil for depression and nervousness.

Bergamot to relieve tension and depression.

Chamomile to soothe dry sensitive skin; it has a relaxing, calming effect.

Clary Sage for nerves, panic and depression.

Eucalyptus and **lemon** are great for breaking up colds, bronchial congestion and relieving muscular aches and pains.

Frankincense helps prevent nightmares and asthma.

Geranium relaxes.

Juniper releases tension.

Lavender for insomnia, headaches, pains, anxiety, panic and depression.

Marjoram for insomnia, anxiety, aches and pains.

Neroli is a good antidepressant and relaxes.

Orange, **geranium** and **lime** calm, settle tempers and help with insomnia.

Pine enhances and deepens breathing, easing sinus problems and influenza.

Rose helps relieve stress and headaches and it is a good antidepressant.

Rosemary improves the memory.

Thyme, **pine**, **lavender** and **eucalyptus** are good air fresheners for stale rooms.

Ylang Ylang helps with depression, relaxes and helps with insomnia.

Aromatic recipes

Anxiety and depression

This blend helps relieve tension, aches and pains, sleeping problems and other symptoms of anxiety.

Lemon grass 10 drops
Jasmine 20 drops
Lime 10 drops
Mandarin 10 drops

Blend with 100 ml carrier oil, for example apricot kernel oil, and massage into the skin. Alternatively add 2 drops cedarwood, 1 drop lemon grass and 2 drops of lavender to your bath water.

The common cold

This blend will relieve symptoms like fever, aches, sore throat, and tiredness.

Black pepper 10 drops
Lemon 10 drops
Tea tree 20 drops
Thyme 10 drops

Blend with 100 ml carrier oil, for example rosehip oil, and massage into the skin. Or add 1 drop each of eucalyptus, peppermint, lime and tea tree to a half-filled bowl of hot water. Place a towel over your head and inhale the vapour for about 10 minutes. Keep your head about 20 cm from the bowl.

For other wonderful blends I suggest you read Judith White's *Aromatherapy, Blends for Life*. Aromatherapy sets the mood and environment for all our alternative therapies. Our next topic, Australian Bush Flower Essences, also delves into the senses.

3
AUSTRALIAN BUSH FLOWER ESSENCES

Nature's gifts are many. All you have to do is stand in the open countryside and absorb nature's healing for the moment.

This morning I was trying to decide what to write about in the next chapter when two funny things happened. Firstly, during my meditation I asked what I should write about. The words 'Australian Bush Flower Essences' came back to me like a ton of bricks. As the morning wore on I changed my mind and began thinking about other things. Later when I checked my mail I found a letter from a young man I had met in Melbourne. This young man has been diagnosed with cancer and I have been helping him work through his emotions using alternative therapies. In the first paragraph of his letter he wrote, 'What can you tell me about the Australian Bush Flower Essences?' My direction for the day was made clear to me. So . . . for my friend in Melbourne and for all those in search of a way to improve your mental, physical and spiritual wellbeing, here is the chapter on Australian Bush Flower Essences.

Passion and purpose helping so many across the world

I had the great pleasure and honour of meeting Ian White, the founder of Australian Bush Flower Essences and author of the book *Australian Bush Flower Essences*, when he invited me to one of his workshops, which was very informative and great fun. Ian is a fifth generation herbalist who has been practising as a naturopath and homoeopath for over fifteen years. He is dedicated to his work and his passion rubs off on those he meets. Everyone I know who has had contact with Ian speaks very highly of both him and his work.

As with everything, I started my research into the Australian Bush Flower Essences with my usual scepticism. Now my family use the Bush Flower Essences for all sorts of things and I carry at least two bottles with me everywhere I go. The results are outstanding.

What flowers are trying to tell you

The ancient Egyptians, Asians, Europeans and South Americans used flower essences. Australian Aborigines still work with flowers to heal emotional and physical states. The Australian bush is full of magnificent flowers and bushes with healing qualities. And flowers have a language of their own.

There are 62 Australian Bush Flower Essences which can be combined to make up other essences, each one made from flowers grown in Australia. Meditation and answers from a higher source have led Ian to know which flower is needed for healing specific feelings and emotions. Even the location where flowers were grown is important. The essences are made from flowers that have their own special vibration helping us to get in touch with our inner self. They deal with the cause rather than the outer physical symptom and help heal negative belief patterns that are held in our subconscious.

Each flower is carefully selected, and then asked permission to be used. All are treated with great reverence and an acknowledgement of the greatness and wonder of nature. Is it any wonder that they are so powerful? Australian Bush Flower Essences can be used to complement treatments for all sorts of things from building self-esteem to dealing with dyslexia, eczema, coughs, bed wetting, anorexia, and much more.

Using the essences

When I was first introduced to these essences I purchased just one bottle, but after learning more about what they can do and enjoying some outstanding results I started working with them more and more. The essences are made from the flowers which are soaked in purified water. The mother essence is mixed with brandy which acts as a preservative. The flower essences are available individually. A single essence is a powerful treatment for a particular condition. For example, Illawarra Flame Tree addresses the fear of responsibility or an overwhelming sense of rejection. The positive outcome you can achieve is increased confidence, commitment, strength, self-reliance and self-approval.

When there is more than one symptom to be dealt with essences can be mixed. For example, a mixture of Bottlebrush and Boronia is used for breaking addictions: that is habits (Bottlebrush) and mental obsessions (Boronia). The positive outcome gives clarity of mind, mental calmness, serenity, ability to cope and carry on. Some essences are made up of several flowers, such as the Emergency Essence which I use when my children are anxious, need calming, fall over or have a headache. I use this essence myself when I am stressed or overloaded with challenges. Sometimes I take it when I am about to face a situation that I know will be tough, to help me remain calm and serene. My children use Emergency Essence when their school work becomes too much especially around exam time. They also use it when they are upset or need pacifying.

The remedies take effect immediately after taking seven drops of the mixture under the tongue, morning and night. For the drops to work really effectively Ian recommends this dose is taken every day for 2–4 weeks. If your children don't want to take them orally you can rub the essences on their wrists, temples or chakra areas. My youngest daughter preferred them in her bath water or in my massage oil when I pampered her. The drops can also be placed on the point where the line from each ear joins at the top of the head.

The number 7

Seven is a very important number and has a special significance in the process of taking these essences. Seven correlates with many aspects of nature in our lives. For example, our lives have seven-year cycles, rain forms in a seven-process cycle and the number seven has great spiritual significance. In numerology, if your number is seven you are very spiritual. If you are missing a number seven in your name it can mean you lack spirituality and consideration. Taking seven drops at a time balances your emotional, physical and spiritual levels with nature.

When treating more than one condition it is important to determine which condition needs to be treated first. Sometimes the essences bring up very strong emotions so it may be wise to take a break from the treatment for a day or so before continuing with the course. But remember these treatments should not replace the services of a doctor or other qualified health professional. If the treatment continues to be too emotional, seek further professional help or assistance.

Because I have a daughter with dyslexia and learning difficulties I was particularly interested to find out how and why the Australian Bush Flower Essences have such outstanding results with these children. After talking with a therapist about our particular challenge, it was suggested that my daughter try Bush Fuchsia which gives clarity in the spoken word and helps integrate the male and female sides, the right and left hemispheres of the brain and the back and front of the brain. Even my daughter was amazed at the difference it made to her outlook and her performance. She seemed more focused and more alert which helped build her confidence. She seemed less fearful of situations involving school work because her mind and thoughts were clearer.

Australian Bush Flower Essences are so powerful they help children who have been traumatised, have fear of fires, have been burnt, or who are or have been involved with drugs and alcohol. They are also helping children (and adults) through the trauma of marriage or relationship breakdown, by dealing with the emotions involved; for example fear, anger, letting go, guilt and dealing with change. There are times when children find it difficult to express their feelings and emotions, so Ian created the Flannel Flower Essence which helps children to open up, face and deal with what is happening in a positive way.

Decisions . . . which essence to choose?

Some people add all of the essences they need in together. But how do you decide which is the correct or priority essence for you or your children? There are many ways including using your own or your children's intuition. You may ask yourselves which essence you or your children feel drawn to. You can ask in meditation and listen for the answer. Alternatively, place an essence of your choice before them and observe your children's reactions. Observe how your children respond to different essences by reading their body language. Talk to your children and ask them what they feel they need. What is their priority? You might like to try dowsing or using a pendulum. A Kinesiology or Kinergetic treatment may provide you with further insight about which essences you need. Or have an iridologist read your eyes.

Questions you may like to ask your children to help you choose the right essences

- What is the situation they want to rectify? Is it physical, mental or spiritual?
- What emotions do they feel when they are in this situation?
- What feelings and emotions do they try to hide when in this situation?
- What do they want to achieve from dealing with this situation?

Make a note of all the feelings and emotions your children bring up and then try to assess the main priorities. The feelings and emotions they are trying to suppress are the ones that need to be brought out into the open and treated. As I have said before, nothing is ever given to us that we cannot deal with, but when working with children or in circumstances when the emotions run deep a gentle approach is essential.

When you have decided on a treatment for your children you might like to take the essence too. In this way you can heal your own inner being at the same time. Remember, to heal the child—you must heal the parent.

Australian Bush Flower Essences can be used by anybody, of any nationality as long as the person using them has positive feelings towards Australia. Some people use the Bach Flower remedies, an English flower remedy founded in the 1930s by Edward Bach, a medical doctor who practised homoeopathy. I use the Australian Bush Flower Essences for my family, but it is for you to determine for yourself which suits you as both treatments have shown incredible results across the world with all sorts of people. You will be drawn to the one that suits your family's needs.

Kirstin

Kirstin was overcoming an addiction and was having to face and deal with emotions she had suppressed for many years. One emotion she found very difficult to acknowledge was resentment and anger. When she was young she was brought up believing that nice girls don't lose their temper and don't resent people. When she was married her husband constantly told her that she was overly emotional, negative and resentful of people, so she tried very hard to hide all her negative emotions especially anger.

Kirstin had never thought of herself as an angry person until, after about two months of counselling, resentment kept surfacing in many different situations. She tried desperately to suppress her feelings, not with drugs or alcohol, but by taking Australian Bush Flower Essences to help build her self-esteem and love for herself. Then one day, in a counselling session, she was told to accept her feelings and that it was okay to express her anger if done in a positive way. She started to treat herself with Dagger Hakea and noticed improvements immediately. Her resentments began to dissipate and she was able to deal with emotional situations without losing her personal power.

Australian Bush Flower Essences are completely natural. They only give you what you need at this moment. If you use an essence and nothing happens, you may need to choose another remedy for a different emotion, one that you need to address first rather than the one you have chosen.

Using these flower essences will help your family have more clarity in what they do, building their self-esteem, confidence and direction. I have included suggestions for essences in each chapter of Part One to help you through different situations or emotions you or your children may experience.

After all my research and work with the Australian Bush Flower Essences I am intensely aware of their power and energy. If I see a flower and I feel it affecting me, I stop and sense what it is giving me. Sometimes when I am alone I'll talk to a flower to see what it wishes to tell me. Take time to sit among different flowers, walk through gardens or the countryside and feel them touch your inner soul. Experience the wealth and beauty of nature. Become one with nature and balance yourself with it.

The next chapter is dedicated to recording what is happening in your life so that you can learn from each action and reaction. You will find it useful to record your feeling when using different essences.

4
JOURNAL YOUR LIFE'S JOURNEY

When the written word is honest and true it releases the soul trapped within.

All these tools for intuitive parenting will probably appear in your journal as they change your way of living. I have kept many journals over the years and have great fun looking back at what has happened and how life has affected me. My personal notes help me realise how much I have grown and how I have reacted differently to situations in the past. Journalling is a way of recording what happens in our lives and how we dealt with challenges at the time. It is a great way of reviewing our lives, finding out what worked, what didn't and why.

Everything that happens in our lives happens for a reason . . . do we really need to go on making the same mistakes? Do we have room in our lives for change? Children need to look at their mistakes and be taught how to learn from them. Journalling helps them examine their lives in order to find patterns that are repeated and can be changed if they so desire.

A journal is only to be shared with others when the owner gives their permission. It is a very special book that, if written properly and with the right intentions, holds many thoughts, feelings and emotions special to the person who has written or drawn them. Because this book is so personal, it needs to be chosen by its owner. Some children may choose a book with a certain colour or design on it that makes them feel good about putting all their thoughts and feelings in it. Some children may want a book with a lock on it for their own peace of mind.

A journal can be used for many reasons and in many ways. Some children like to write, some like to draw, some might do both. Some may even be artistic enough to use collage, paste in photos, pictures, tickets, or even put special letters in it. The idea of a journal is for children to record their thoughts, feelings, emotions, the situations they have been in, people they have met or dealt with, how they dealt with them, their dreams and goals, and memories both good and bad. When children find themselves in a similar situation to one they have been in before a journal is a great resource. They can see how they acted and reacted previously and make a decision on how to deal with the situation this time round.

A journal is meant to be a very private and intimate record of the soul's journey. It is a place of self-disclosure, openness and truth to the self. Some journallers find writing in their journal difficult at first, as it delves deep into the soul, but with more practice and regular entries journallers find that words begin to flow and an original piece of work is created. I know that sometimes when I start to write I am a bit hesitant, but as the words flow onto the paper they appear to come together and make sense, giving me clarity, and I get a real sense of peace as I offload my thoughts. Somehow, writing thoughts and feelings down makes your worries seem less heavy or depressing. Writing doesn't solve problems but it does unjumble the situation and the writer is able to see a new direction, shifting their focus into a more positive mode.

Encourage your children to keep a journal and to take time every day to write or draw something about their day.

When my children go on holidays or travel I get them to keep a journal to record their experiences. Recently I was given one of my daughter's journals to read. She had written it on her trip to England. She was eleven and had travelled alone. It was her first big trip without Mum. She felt very homesick and wrote us all little messages which came to her when she was unable to contact us by phone. She found that writing her feelings down in her special book helped relieve the pain of being away from her family.

When my family travelled around Australia for eight months, we each kept a journal. These were great to read afterwards. Although we had all shared the same journey, we all experienced situations in our own unique way. Journalling makes children very aware of who they really are and what makes them tick. They become more observant and more creative, and journalling helps with their writing and reading skills. When journalling, include descriptions of situations, people, reactions and actions, detailing all emotions and feelings, positive and negative. When you look back over your journal, you will recognise patterns in your behaviour, and you and your children will be able to choose whether the same action or reaction should be replayed or dealt with in a different way.

Glenda

Glenda, a woman I know, always keeps a journal, but it took some time and two disastrous marriages before a particular pattern she kept repeating became apparent to her. Her love relationships always had the same outcome, disaster. As she read over previous diaries she realised that she was continually being attracted to the same sort of man—good looking, charming, romantic, a 'knight in shining armour', with no commitment once the pursuit was over. She realised that all the bunches of roses, expensive dinners and theatre outings had simply aroused in her feelings of being wanted and needed by someone. She learnt that she no longer needed to fulfil these feelings because she found an inner peace within herself which finally drew the right relationship to her.

As children find out about themselves through their journal they will discover more about their likes and dislikes. One young woman's journal was full of boys' names. What they wore, what they did and said. Against these comments she wrote what she liked, what she didn't and why.

When our emotions become heated and frayed a journal is a great place to release anger and fear. By writing them down on paper the conflicts and challenging situations don't seem to hard and our anger seems to dissipate. If you or your children are angry with someone or at something write a letter to the person or about the situation. Say what you really feel. The letter isn't meant to be sent or read by anyone else but writing it all down helps you release and let go of the anger. In some circumstances you may find what has been written or drawn is a valuable piece of information to discuss with a counsellor or therapist if the problem is not resolving itself.

Journalling is also a great way to record the dreams we have in our sleep. Our dreams hold many of the answers we need in our everyday life. Many of us forget our dreams as soon as we wake up. Keep your journal by the side of your bed so that as soon as you wake up you can record your dreams and your feelings about them. Another good reason to leave your journal by your bed is if you are having difficulty sleeping. When we worry about situations or people we may find it difficult to go to sleep. Write all your thoughts and worries down in your journal and you'll find you soon go to sleep.

In an earlier chapter I discussed setting goals. Get your children to record their goals in their journal. It is a great place for them to write down everything they want in detail. If they are making regular entries in their journal they will see their goals written there too, which will reinforce their dreams.

I have a help page in my journal. This includes things that can help me, like positive affirmations or sayings and the phone numbers of people I can contact if the situation I am in gets too hard for me to cope alone. This is extremely important if your children are going through a really bad time.

Some people keep their journal as a memory keepsake to be able to look back on relationships or situations that have been very special. Reading about the good times can lift your spirit when your life is at a low ebb. Love letters are often kept in journals. Being very private and personal they can make readers feel loved and cared for even if the relationship is no longer. I still transfer a telegram sent from England to Austria by a boyfriend I had when I was fifteen, from one journal to another. It reminds me of my first real love. A time that was very special to me.

On a more serious note, journals are also important to keep when you or anyone in your family is going through a challenging time like separation, or are recovering from an abusive situation. Journals can be used to record dates, times, places, people and conversations which can later be used as evidence of what happened.

Setting up your journal

Once your writers have chosen their own book they will need to prepare it to suit their needs. Setting up your journal can be as easy as you like, especially for little children. You may like to put in a page with the following headings to guide your children in their writing.

- Today I achieved . . .
- Today I enjoyed. . .
- Today I didn't like . . . because . . .
- I felt like . . . today
- My sister/brother/mum/dad/made me feel . . .
- My goal for this week is . . .
  and so on.

There is so much that can be put into a journal whatever size it is—remember it holds a life. The next chapter discusses Kinergetics, a therapy I have had the most fun with. I was very sceptical in the beginning but many sessions later I truly believe that this therapy works miracles.

5
KINERGETICS

We are who we are today because our mind, body and soul have stored every thought, deed and reaction away in a memory bank for future events.

The body doesn't lie

The previous chapter about journalling helped us release our feelings through the written word. Kinergetics helps release energy imbalances so we can deal with challenging situations and feelings in a more successful way. Kinergetics is a form of Kinesiology that helps improve the health by rebalancing the body's flow of energy through muscle testing. Dr. George Goodheart discovered muscle testing in the 1960s. He linked Western medical science with ancient Chinese therapies to create a natural energy flow in the body. Every emotive incident in our lives is stored in our bodies and even though we may try to deny certain thoughts, feelings, emotions or memories, muscle testing identifies them and assists in releasing the suppressed emotion.

I want to acknowledge the enormous difference to my life that Dave 'The Plumber' Everett has made. Dave is a Kinergetics practitioner. When I first heard about his work I was very sceptical, but having received the benefit of his treatment

I highly recommend Kinergetics. Dave is unblocking people's emotional lives through Kinergetics. It is one of the most exciting alternative therapies I have found.

When we talk ourselves into adopting a certain belief which is, in fact, in conflict with our belief system it causes us both internal and external conflict and stress. We also lie to ourselves. For example, you may say to yourself, 'I deserve to be happy within a beautiful, loving relationship,' but because of past events you have suppressed your true feelings and now you don't really believe this statement. During muscle testing these lies will surface when you have the desire to face them and deal with them. We have all experienced situations and events that happen over and over again because we haven't learnt from them last time round. How many relationships do we fall into, thinking they are different from the last one? The cover may be different, but inside the story is the same. Kinergetics helps you face these emotions and accept how they have affected you in the past. This therapy helps you acknowledge, release and let go of the emotions that are blocking you from moving on and being successful in life.

How it works

A practitioner can work with their client standing up, sitting or lying down. The client is then asked to hold their arm out from their body and keep it steady. The practitioner applies a light pressure to the client's wrist while asking the client questions. If the client tells the truth his arm will stay firm. If the client lies the muscles in the arm will relax. In this way imbalances, both emotional and physical, and self-sabotage impulses are detected. Self-sabotage impulses are emotions that have been repressed and are waiting to be released. The practitioner will then ascertain from the body how it wants to be re-balanced through treatments like affirmations, Australian Bush Flower

Essences, vitamins, diet, simple exercises, chakra healing, organ healing and so on.

My experience

The first time I went to see Dave, my Kinergetics practitioner, I went not knowing what to expect, but I was open to trying a new therapy. I had many things that I knew had to be dealt with, but the discovery that most surprised me was the fact that fear of success was blocking my life in every area. I was shocked. I couldn't understand how I could be frightened of success. The session established how I had sabotaged many situations in my life; when I was given statements about success to read out I fumbled and stuttered. My head thought one thing but my body said something else. After a couple of hours' treatment I was able to say the statement without faltering. Events after the session helped me realise that the blockages had been removed.

Life experience . . . sometimes the truth hurts

We all go through situations in our lives designed to help us grow. Some of these experiences are frightening, scary, stressful, exciting and nerve-racking. We have the choice to look at them honestly and openly or hide them away. And as frightening as it may sound most children experience sexual, physical, and mental abuse in some form in their young lives.

Leonie

When I first met Leonie she was suffering from low self-esteem, poor appetite, nervousness, fearfulness, anger, guilt and lack of confidence. She had just left a relationship which had been mentally abusive, and she felt worthless. She sought help from a Kinergetics practitioner, and muscle testing brought up other similar experiences. She had experienced mental or physical abuse in other situations and each left her with the feeling that she was useless and worthless. In one such incident she had been physically abused at the age of six by a neighbour. Many of the emotions and trauma from these situations had been suppressed as she had not told anyone for fear of shame and recrimination.

From this one experience she continued to create situations in which she was the victim. Each situation was a chance to change, to break the pattern, but she hadn't taken the opportunity because she didn't know why it was happening. Finally Leonie reached a point where her body and spirit were telling her to regain control of her life and her personal power. It was time for Leonie to be productive and successful. Kinergetics helped her to see the patterns and unblocked her emotions.

Kinergetics deals with the emotions that cause physical ailments and sensitivities. It can help to detect sensitivities and allergies to certain foods or metals; balance immune dysfunction; relieve back pain; overcome learning difficulties, or anxieties and phobias. Kinergetics is often used to help heal sport and fitness injuries, or provide relief from headache, digestion problems, depression, tiredness, and vitamin and mineral deficiencies.

Kinergetics and Attention Deficit Disorder (ADD)

Are you aware that children who have ADD tend to rock in their chair? This action helps them to link their left and right brain which makes them more focused and productive. Children who suffer from ADD are missing this link, but Brain Gym, a form of Kinesiology, introduces children to exercises that help them bridge that gap. Kinergetics is highly effective in helping release the emotions causing children with ADD to behave in self-destructive ways.

Physical exercises to help children with ADD

1. Ask your child to draw a lazy figure eight on a piece of paper, in the air, or in her mind. She must try to make the figure eight as symmetrical as possible.
2. Cross crawl exercise—Ask your child to march on the spot, lifting her knees high. Then with her left arm crossed over her body, ask her to touch her right knee with her left hand and vice-versa. Make sure she doesn't bring her legs across to meet her body.
3. Marching—She should march forward with her head held high and straight. Ask her to swing her arms and lift her legs up, all as straight as possible.
4. Put her head on her shoulder and with her arm outstretched, ask her to draw a figure eight in the air.

I tried all these exercises with my daughter and found them to be extremely beneficial especially when used with other therapies.

You might like to try the following allergy test at home with your children. It is very simple.

1. Stand or sit opposite your child or partner.
2. Get them to hold one arm out at 45 degrees from their body.
3. Place two fingers on top of their wrist while they push their arm against your fingers. They should be able to resist you gently without fighting you.
4. Put the food you want to test in front of your child's third eye, chest or in their hand and repeat the third step to see if they can hold their arm firm.

5. If they are unable to keep their arm firm they may be allergic to that food or substance. The change in arm movement may be only very slight but with practice you will be able to notice the change.

Please note that Kinergetics and Kinesiology, as well as many other alternative therapies, have not been scientifically proven. For an accurate diagnosis of an allergy or underlying medical condition you must consult your doctor. If you are not sure what sort of treatment your children need you can use Kinergetics to find out. Remember that the body doesn't lie. It knows what it wants and cries out for it. Get in touch with your body and listen to what it wants for a healthier, more productive way of living.

Our bodies cry out for love and attention, especially when overworked or abused. The next therapy we explore is massage to help you and your children relax in mind, body and spirit.

6
MASSAGE GIVES THE MESSAGE

The touch of fingertips gently massages our emotions into awareness.

We have been looking at therapies that give us ways to heal ourselves and our children. All of these therapeutic tools are wonderful to experience as a family, and massage is great for building healthy relationships and bonds.

Our society is interested in natural childbirth. When the baby is born it is placed immediately on the mother's bare stomach and then encouraged to breastfeed. Both of these things are meant to help create a strong bond between parent and child. Although bonding doesn't always happen instantly, it is the first step. We all want someone to hold us and tell us that we are okay when we are sad or hurt. It feels good when someone throws their arms around us in times of triumph, or holds our hands when we need to be guided or led. Physical contact is important for you and your children to create a bond in your relationship.

Everyone wants to be loved, wanted and needed, and as children we want to be cuddled and pampered. A hug is free. It is something that we all want and need. It makes us and the people we interact with feel good as we exchange energy. Children respond well to affection, but unfortunately we tend to shy away from touching, cuddling and kissing other people and children, isolating ourselves from the affection we crave. Something may have happened in our childhood that stops us from being affectionate and demonstrative with our own children. To break through the limitations and boundaries we have created we need to try to do things in a different way.

Recent research suggests that massage as a healing technique was used as far back as 3000 BC. Today we use massage therapy to relax and heal. As I have said, massage is a very good way to bond with your children so start as soon as you can—it is never too late. Babies love to be touched. Their eyes sparkle, their bodies respond to your touch and they get goosebumps. Massage shows them how much you love and care for them. The more you touch babies the more touchy-feely they are as children, teenagers and adults, and they seem to have fewer inhibitions about physical contact.

In some Eastern countries, massage is an ancient custom passed on from mother to daughter. Many tribal and nomadic women carry their children next to their body in a sling or on their back while carrying on with their everyday activities. This closeness helps them to get to know one another intimately.

Massage releases tension and stress and, when done before bedtime, helps children go to sleep. A massage before bed is particularly good for hyperactive children, children who worry or those who have difficulty going off to sleep. One client I had was a 10-year-old boy who was experiencing great difficulty going to sleep, so much so he dreaded even going into his bedroom.

His parents had recently separated and he was having trouble with his relationships at school, so he had many anxious thoughts. I suggested that he make his bedroom a safe haven for himself. He needed to make it a place where he could relax. He agreed, and went about making changes to his room to make it his own castle.

His mother bought him some new bedsheets that he really wanted. He changed things around. He threw out a lot of rubbish which helped him unclutter his life, and placed things where he wanted. I suggested that his mother got him an aromatherapy burner with some oils and a specific massage oil to help him deal with his emotions. When he walked into his room at night he lit a couple of candles and his aromatherapy burner, and he made sure his meditation tape was ready to play after his massage. As he lay down on the bed he took three deep breaths and tried to relax.

His mother spent 15 minutes every evening massaging him. When she finished, she kissed him goodnight and turned on his meditation tape very quietly. Quite often her son was asleep before she had finished but she still turned the tape on so the positive message could reach his subconscious self. After just a few days the young boy was waking up refreshed, feeling easier in his mind, body and spirit. His confidence grew and he seemed much calmer in everything he did.

Massage can help children with muscular tension, especially children who grind their teeth. By massaging their facial muscles you relax them which releases any stored tension. Massage can also help with menstrual pains, cramps, headaches and constipation. It is great for reducing bed wetting and sleepwalking. Massage helps children get in touch with and become aware of their own bodies. Because massage is a one-on-one activity it has positive effects for you too. It can be treated as a special time for you and your children. If you work it right, your children will be more than happy to reciprocate with a massage.

But please note, if your children have been subjected to physical abuse then extra care needs to be taken. Your children should only be touched when they are ready and they may have to learn the art of touching all over again, regaining trust and acceptance.

There are many different massage techniques you may like to investigate and try. The following guidelines can apply to any massage technique or you may simply let your children and your hands guide you.

- If your children feel happy for you to touch their skin, make sure your hands are warm. If your children have reservations about you touching their skin, massage through their clothing. It is just as effective.
- Soft relaxing music will set the scene and atmosphere, also make sure that the room is warm enough for your children to be exposed to the night air.
- Massage oil feels really lovely on the skin so use a cold pressed vegetable oil that will moisturise the skin. Choose a massage oil for their specific needs and treatment or add some Australian Bush Flower Essences to the oil. Oil poured straight from the bottle can be cold and might give young babies or children a shock. Pour the oil onto your hands to warm it first.
- When giving a massage it is important that you work on both sides of the body for the body to stay centred and balanced and make sure you have the time to complete what you start even if it is only five minutes. When first starting with babies massage them very gently with only your fingertips and as they grow older gradually increase your touch. Stroke each area of the body two or three times. With older children go with your intuition but ask them how it feels and see how they respond to your touch. You can use your fingertips or your whole hand depending on where you are massaging.
- To give a whole body massage start at the top of their head, move down the face, across the neck, shoulders, arms, torso, stomach, legs and then the feet. Finish the front of the body with long gentle strokes all the way down the body. Then get your children to turn over and massage from the head, down the neck, the back, over

the bottom and down the legs to the feet. Again finish off with long gentle strokes from the head right down the body to the toes.

- For just a head, neck, and shoulders massage, start at the top and work down. But don't massage babies in this manner and never massage a baby's head. Remember their bones are still forming and they need the most gentle of touches.
- Your children may even enjoy a foot or hand massage. Their little bodies will respond to your touch. With practice you will find you will be able to read the signs and know where to massage and with what strength. Of course you should never massage over the spine, or broken bones and if your children have a skin condition consult your doctor first.

Quite often as I massage my children I ask them to quietly go within themselves and ask their own bodies where they need special attention. The body stores emotions in different places and so one part of their body may need more attention than another. I also ask my children what colour they feel they need. After they have asked their own body for a colour, I ask them to fill their whole body with that colour. They go into a highly relaxed state. I used to stroke one child's face with my thumb to help him relax and go to sleep, now when he gets really tired he strokes his face with his own thumb. It soothes and relaxes him. He finds that he strokes his face during exam times because it comforts him in his time of stress.

A highly effective massage is best achieved with sensitive touch and love. Your hands will pass on the message. Share a massage with your children when you are relaxed yourself. If you find the art of touching or being touched difficult, you may need to work on releasing the fear of touch through meditation.

You may want to begin with other ways to massage and relax your children such as brushing their hair and playing with it. Brushing massages and revitalises the scalp. Quite often we sit watching television and play with each other's hair. It's very comforting. Try scratching their backs. As the saying goes, you scratch mine and I'll scratch yours—a great game. Get your family to line up and scratch each other's back, then turn around and scratch the back of the person that has scratched you, or if your family is big enough form a circle. You can draw or write on their backs with your fingers, making a good guessing game. Sometimes we massage each other's hands and feet especially after a heavy day of writing or sporting activities. It seems to revitalise the parts of our bodies that are overworked.

A warm shower is a good way to massage yourself when there is no one else to do it for you. Stand in the jets of warm water and let them massage your body where you are aching or have pain. Music is also a great way to massage the soul. There are times when we need complete silence which is also healing, and then there are times when certain music will caress our feelings and emotions into wellbeing. Whichever method you use it is a lovely way to end the day.

In the next chapter we are going to learn about meditation which can help relax your children even more—if that's possible. You can use meditation music while you are massaging and complete your treatment with a positive meditation to reinforce successful ways of living.

7
MEDITATION

The art of being quiet and still.

Self-medication

We have just relaxed the body through massage, now we are going to delve into the conscious and subconscious mind using meditation.

You can do it with your eyes open or shut; sitting upright or lying down; on top of a mountain or in a shed. You can do it alone, one on one, or in a group situation. It is extremely important to take the time to make a regular habit of meditating, focusing all your thoughts and energies within.

When we search within we realise our own potential and understand that we possess the answers to our questions about life within the mind, body and soul. We realise that we can face life's challenges, creating our reality and becoming aware of our inner wisdom, our intuition.

All of us meditate at various times throughout the day, mostly unconsciously, as our thoughts drift to peaceful things, such as a sunset, a beautiful flower, passing clouds, or even a wistful daydream. Children are experts at daydreaming, and yet we ask them to stop.

Meditation has been and is being used by people from all

walks of life, across the world. The positive advantages of meditation are being realised now in the West and various techniques and practices are being introduced into schools, hospitals, homes and even the workplace.

Having done many forms of meditation myself over the years, I have adapted my own methods that also suit my children. I usually meditate first thing in the morning when I wake up. It is a quiet time before the children get up for school. I stay quietly in bed, lying flat with my arms down by my sides and the palms facing up. I then centre my being by taking a few deep breaths and allow myself to become aware of peace and tranquillity within my body. I take this time to acknowledge my higher power or my guides, asking for guidance and courage to face and deal with the day ahead in a way that will serve my highest purpose. I use this as my prayer time as well as asking what I need to know. I listen and watch what is given to me in the way of messages or pictures. I then thank my higher power, take a deep breath, stretch my limbs and gently get out of bed. Some people cannot lie down to meditate because they fall asleep, so sitting in an upright position is equally as good.

Sometimes I use a tape to listen to as I am meditating which guides me along the theme I want to address. When meditating with my children I sit by them as they lie in bed and I guide them with the story. Sometimes when we are walking we will stop and sit to absorb nature's beauty and meditate quietly in the open air. I also guide my children in a brief meditation just before they go into exams.

Because I have had such dramatic results in my own life through meditation, creative visualisation and positive thinking, I have brought my children up to experience the benefits of meditation for themselves and within the family. The results are astounding. Children are very imaginative and although they can be quite scattered in their thoughts they can learn to focus their thoughts on a successful activity. Many schools are using meditation to teach children to have more positive attitudes, giving them skills to help them take more responsibility for their own lives. Teachers are realising the importance of using meditation and relaxation techniques in the classroom to help children cope with stress and focus on learning.

After spending many years in the field of motivation and training, it is wonderful to see the corporate world using meditation and relaxation techniques and reaping the benefits. But why should our children wait until they have grown up to enjoy these benefits? Children are very receptive to meditation and enjoy it. It is wonderful to hear children talk about what they have experienced in their meditations and creative picture-building sessions.

What meditation can do for your children

By teaching your children to make some time in their day to meditate you are helping them to focus and acknowledge their thoughts and energies; helping them to get in touch with their real needs and discover that the answers lie within. Meditation helps them to create and achieve their goals and dreams, giving them direction and purpose. It helps them to take responsibility for their actions.

Meditation can help your children to learn the art of being quiet and still; to go within and recognise the beauty of the self, nature and the universe. Through meditation they can learn to trust their inner knowledge and turn positive thoughts, emotions and goals into reality. Using positive affirmations or positive self talk they can heal their bodies and souls through meditation practices. Meditation also helps them to face and deal with life's stresses and challenges by releasing and letting go of negatives and replacing them with positives. They learn to face their fears and free themselves from limitations which builds their self-esteem, developing a real loving for themselves, valuing their worth as the magnificent human beings they really are.

Through their meditations they will meet their guides or guardians on whom they can call for help and guidance at any time, which will expand and develop in them a stronger awareness and more intuitive way of living. The more they meditate and centre themselves, the more grounded and balanced they will feel. Their energy will flow, bringing them into the here and now, which is especially important when used in the classroom situation or in times of stress.

When is it best to meditate and for how long?

Some children prefer to meditate in the morning just as they are getting up, and others choose to meditate at night when they go to bed, but if they have a special event, for example a competition, carnival or an exam, meditating just before the event is most advantageous. Meditating in the morning will focus and prepare your children for the rest of the day, whereas meditating in the evening before bed helps them to bless the activities of the day and go to sleep in a positive mood.

Meditation is also beneficial when your children feel out of balance or scared, or if they have a particular problem they need help with. Just going and sitting in a quiet place such as a park, in the school library or on the beach will help them reach the answers they need and move on.

What time of day is best for meditation will vary according to what is going on in your children's lives and what suits their needs. I had a phone call recently from Judy, a very distressed mother, who uses my meditation tape 'It's Cool to be Kidz' for her son who is hyperactive and has ADD. She said that her 8-year-old son, Troy, would not go to bed until midnight and was not settled enough to listen to the tape. Instead, she plays the tape in the morning just as Troy is waking up. The results have been phenomenal. His attitude and his actions have changed dramatically. Troy's teachers have even commented on the change in his behaviour and his receptiveness to school work. He appears to be more focused, able to get himself ready for what lies ahead, and more open to suggestion.

In a classroom situation, teachers find that getting the children to meditate after lunch is a great help. A headmaster rang me to congratulate my work because he had gone into a Year One class after lunch when, he said, they were usually still climbing the walls, and found the class all lying flat on the floor totally engrossed in their meditation journey. He went back ten minutes later and, he said, 'They were still there! Congratulations.' The teacher of this class had used meditation at a time that was most advantageous for the children and herself.

Many schools are using meditation after playtime or lunch to get children to focus their thoughts back on the class and the work at hand. Five minutes of meditation before a class starts links a child's left and right brain, focusing thoughts, and making the child more receptive to information as well as retaining more. It's easy to see why school marks improve with regular use of meditation. Hopefully meditation will soon be on the school timetable.

Whether your children meditate for five minutes a day or for half an hour doesn't matter, it's the regular practice that is the most important factor.

What's age got to do with it?

When I first introduced my children to meditation, my youngest was two and a half years old. While my other two children would lie down and close their eyes, concentrating on the story, the little one would jump out of bed to go to the toilet, or teddy would fall out of bed and a great scurry would eventuate because teddy would get lost in all the other things under her bed. But one day she recounted a wonderful experience she had with the animals in her meditation. That encouraged her to go in search of more experiences which have helped develop and fine-tune her intuition.

Many pregnant mothers play my meditation tapes to the child within. Day care centres and nursery schools use meditation tapes at rest times, some of the children being nine months to one year old, with outstanding results. Some children won't rest without them.

Meditation is a wonderful gift to teach your children or students whatever age—they are never too young. It is also fantastic for parents and teachers.

Keeping their attention

When I put my tapes together I decided to incorporate a few techniques that would help children use their imagination by building pictures using colour, music, and sound effects; their senses to heighten awareness and intuition; and their thoughts in a positive manner through affirmations and positive statements to enhance their own wellbeing. I wanted to teach children to take time out for themselves, allowing them to learn more about themselves and their emotions. I also wanted to encourage children to use their thought patterns to their fullest, to focus on and give direction to their lives.

Children need to know their emotions are felt and expressed for a reason, and should not be suppressed or used in a negative state. Through meditation they can acknowledge their feelings and emotions, releasing them, letting go and then moving on with their lives.

Meditations for children should be written in such a way that they keep the children focused and interested. I created journeys for my kids to go on in which they were part of the story, meeting up with characters they could relate to. By using lots of colours and descriptions children build wonderful pictures in their minds, which help their creativity. The music has to be special too, to make them feel as though they are on a journey. For teenagers the music has to be more subtle. Music that triggers specific thoughts is advantageous as it enhances the imagination. For example, one tape that I wrote uses music connected to horses and Native American Indians because this is the scene I am setting. Sound association builds pictures making it easier to meditate. After all, teenagers have other things to think about!

Creativity at play

What your children put into their minds may become their reality. By using colours, descriptions and sound effects they build wonderful pictures with powerful, creative energies. When teachers use meditation in class, they follow it with a creative activity such as painting, craft or dance. One teacher told me she had been using one of my meditation tapes on a Year Two class and after the meditation the children each did a painting. Out of a class of twenty-four, twelve of the paintings were selected and sent overseas to a competition where out of 2000 entries three of those twelve paintings were given top awards. Can you imagine the level of self-esteem in that class now?

Life's challenges

Children love meditating if you make it fun. It keeps them focused—so why not get a message of life across at the same time? Meditations can help children cope with daily stresses by keeping them positive, affirming all the great things about themselves, and dispelling negative attitudes and thoughts they may have.

Children take in positive as well as negative information from the moment they are born, so the more positive information we can give them the better off they will be. If they have a problem, meditating can help solve it by reaching their inner being. It can then give them new direction and faith in what they think and do. After a while they discover they have the answers within, which stops them blaming the outside world, and teaches them to trust their inner voice, their intuition.

You can use children's meditations too

Unike Peter Pan many of us lose the child within—we grow up. The emotional challenges adults go through are extensions of their childhood. When adults use my children's meditation tapes they find themselves reaching right in, touching emotions that have been suppressed for many years. You might find this as you work with your children. As with all these therapies, if you can heal yourself, you can also heal your children and those around you. As you go further on this path with your children, your own awareness will expand and your life will grow spiritually, mentally and physically. If you find yourself opening up a Pandora's box of emotions, talk to someone about it or write it down rather than suppressing your feelings and emotions.

One mother was investigating my meditation tape, 'Soul Without the Blues', for her teenage son because it deals with frustration and anger. She stood listening to it on the earphones and her face went white, she clutched her chest and she gasped. She ripped off the earphones and said, 'I'll have to go away and think about this.' About half an hour later she returned. 'I'll have that tape—for me. Nothing has ever affected me like that before. I definitely have some things to work through and that tape has already penetrated right into my chest.'

Another gentleman sat listening to one of my children's meditations and suddenly burst into tears. He'd been badly abused as a child and had kept up a facade to hide his pain.

The particular meditation he was listening to opened up ways for him to heal himself. Remember you will never be given something you cannot cope with.

Healing qualities

Meditation is a wonderful way to heal the mind, body and soul. Many sick people and children are being encouraged by their doctors, teachers, practitioners and counsellors to go to meditation classes to help ease their pain, both physical and mental. Meditation gets the mind in such strong focus that the thoughts received in meditation are much stronger than ordinary thoughts. Positive affirmations and statements are magnified. Adults and children have been known to recover from cancer and other illnesses through thinking themselves healed, using colour, sound and words. One letter I had came from a little 10-year-old boy with Tourette syndrome who has an involuntary tic. He had been using meditation to build his self-esteem and discovered that it also slowed down his tic, and he was able to sleep better as a result.

Bonding

The other wonderful thing that happens when you share meditations with your children is it creates a bond. Meditation takes you somewhere within yourselves that you can share with each other. It also helps you to reject judgemental attitudes as it opens your heart, mind and soul to see yourself for who you really are. When children have problems, we tend to judge them according to our own upbringing, attitudes and perception, but they know what to do if they reach inside themselves and grasp the wisdom of their souls.

Take the time to discuss with your children what happens to them on their journeys. They can repeat the same meditation over and over but the outcome will be different each time as they expand their knowledge. The discussions you have after meditation can be fascinating and great lessons too. Meditation is a wonderful springboard into other areas of self-development. Ongoing self-development is an essential part of life. Your passion for life is fuelled by the beauty in nature and within yourself. Meditation connects you with your inner light and life.

Conclusion

This concludes the seven alternative therapies I have chosen to share with you, although there are many more you may like to investigate for yourself. I have had great pleasure researching, writing and sharing my experiences with you. More than anything I am happy to have been a part of your life. We all have something to share with one another and as we each travel our path I hope we may meet again.

Remember, we are all here such a short time, and our children are only on loan to us. Enjoy the energy your children bring to your life. Enjoy their lives and enhance your own by sharing the different stages of their lives with them. Perhaps there are stages you missed in your life that you can fulfil this time round. Share each moment with gratitude. You are sharing life with another soul. What will you teach them and what will they teach you? Fill each moment with love and be loved. In times of trouble ask for help and you will receive it.

RESOURCES—WE ALL NEED HELP AND SUPPORT

How to choose the right person to turn to for help

Life can be tough at times. The stresses and strains of life can make your problems seem bigger than you can handle. We all need help and we must ask for it when we need it rather than hoping our problems will just disappear. Start by finding the right person or organisation to help with your specific needs. There are many professionals ready to help you. It is up to you to decide which one to choose.

The range of health professionals you can choose from may include: your family doctor, counsellors, psychiatrists, psychologists, psychotherapists, social workers, and nurses. If you belong to a religious organisation or charity you may decide to seek help through that network. You may decide to seek support through an alternative therapy, or use an alternative therapy to complement another form of therapy.

Word of mouth is usually a good way to find a health professional, although what may have worked for someone else may not necessarily work for you or your children. Otherwise you can be referred by your doctor or health professional and if the person you approach thinks they are not the best person to help you, they will refer you on. Some of these people have long waiting lists, but it is worth persevering. Associations can often provide help and advice also.

There are several things that you should take into account when choosing a health professional. Check the professionals' credentials. You will need to check on the cost as well. Will their services be covered under the NHS? If you need help paying fees ask if you can get assistance. Some practitioners will assess you and adjust their fees. When you pay for a service you tend to be more committed to going back for more. Quite often when things are free we get a bit lazy. If possible give some value to the service you are seeking.

You and your children have to get on with this person, so personality is very important. Should you choose someone of the same gender as your child? Sometimes it is worth facing the challenge with a person of the opposite sex to help break down barriers that may have been put up. On the other hand a person of the same sex may help you or your children to feel safe; especially if the reason for seeking treatment concerns sexual abuse.

Check how often you should visit. In the initial stages more help may be needed so more visits may have to be made, but make sure they fit in with your own needs and routine.

Remember, what you say to a professional is confidential, although there are some noted exceptions. Confidentiality can be broken if the professional feels that the person being counselled is of harm to themselves or to others, or if there is any cause to believe the client has or is in contact with an infectious disease, or if the children are under 16 years of age. The years from 14 to 16 years of age are a grey area for professionals, and it is their decision whether confidentiality needs to be broken.

Quite often other members of the family or close friends won't be taken on as clients by the same practitioner.

Remember that you are seeking help and support and time is precious and costly, so make sure that when you go you are prepared. Write down the questions and issues you want to address. Try not to get into small talk. Be truthful and forthright, and try to get the most out of every session.

Sometimes it is advisable to see more than one practitioner for the same problem. In such circumstances it is of the utmost importance the practitioners keep up-to-date with each other.

Whatever you, your children or your family decide to do, no one has to know unless you decide you want to tell them. Choose carefully who you tell and keep it simple, and only tell others as much as you are comfortable telling them.

Support groups for parents and children

Support groups are available no matter what dilemma you may face. You never have to do things on your own. There is always help to be found somewhere. If you don't know where to go, start by ringing one group and they may be able to put you in touch with another. Children's hospitals are also a good resource for information.

Support groups can help you and your children:

- to realise you are not alone—there are others like you.
- to see a light at the end of the tunnel when things are tough.
- to gain direction and feel you are on the right path, and give you guidance on how to change.
- to express and release thoughts. Sharing ideas, thoughts and feelings helps you find other ways of approaching your problems.
- to gain hope and encouragement.
- to hear others talk and share their problems, which may help release some of your own hidden or masked emotions and feelings.
- to feel you are worthy and you deserve the very best.
- to acknowledge you are doing the very best you possibly can for yourself and your children.

How to get the most out of support groups

When you or your children go to self-development classes you can turn the experience into a huge success. While you may feel that some things are pushing you out of your comfort zone, the benefits are worth it. By doing the following, you will get the most out of support groups:

1. Sit near the front.
2. Listen.
3. Always take notes of the talk and include anything that comes to mind during the time.
4. Ask questions and get answers to your satisfaction.
5. Be as honest as you can when you are asked to take part in activities.
6. Always make sure that you are in a group where the information will go no further than inside the room. Usually the facilitator will say this at the beginning of the session to confirm this with you.
7. Each situation will be different because of the environment, topic being worked on, and people around you. Share your emotions. When you express an emotion acknowledge it, release it and let it be. There is no shame in crying or venting your anger.
8. Never be afraid to ask for help or for a clearer explanation of something you don't understand.
9. If you cannot speak out in front of other people within your group see your facilitator during breaks. Your facilitator is there to help you.
10. Read your notes again and take note of how you feel afterwards.
11. Note what changes you can make in your life and make them now.

Support groups

On the following pages is a list of organisations, associations, government departments and support services, with their contact details, for you to use as a starting point.

Bullying Online
Tel: 0207 378 1446
www.bullying.co.uk

ChildLine
45 Folgate Street,
London E1 6GL
Tel: 020 7650 3200
Fax: 020 7650 3201
24-hour helpline: 0800 1111
www.childline.org.uk

Department of Health
Substance Misuse Team
Room 580D Skipton House,
80 London Road
London SE1 6LH
Tel: 020 7972 2000
Fax: 020 7972 1615
www.doh.gov.uk/drugs

Eating Disorders Association
103 Prince of Wales Road,
Norwich NR1 1DW
Adult Helpline: 0845 634 1414
Youthline: 0845 634 7650
www.edauk.com

Gingerbread
London Resource Centre,
Charterhouse,
40 Tabard Street,
London SE1 4JU
Tel: 020 7407 1114
Advice line: 0800 018 4318
www.gingerbread.org.uk

Kidscape
2 Grosvenor Gardens,
London SW1W 0DH
Tel: 020 7730 3300
Fax: 020 7730 7081
www.kidscape.org.uk

'Know the Score'
Scotland's Drugs Information Gateway
Tel: 0800 587 5879
www.knowthescore.info

Mental Health Foundation
83 Victoria Street,
London SW1H 0HW
Tel: 020 7802 0300
Fax: 020 7802 0301
www.mhf.org.uk

Mind (National Association for Mental Health)
15-19 Broadway,
London E15 4BQ
Tel: 020 8519 2122
Fax: 020 8522 1725
Infoline: 0845 766 0163
www.mind.org.uk

National Drugs Helpline
Tel: 0800 776600
www.ndh.org.uk
www.drugs.gov.uk

The 'Frank' Campaign
(for teenagers in England and Wales)
www.talktofrank.com
Email: frank@talktofrank.com

National Family Mediation
Alexander House, Telephone Avenue,
Bristol BS1 4BS
Tel: 0117 904 2825
Fax: 0117 904 3331
www.nfm.u-net.com

NHS Direct
Tel: 0845 4647
www.nhsdirect.nhs.uk

One Parent Families
255 Kentish Town Road,
London NW5 2LX
Tel: 020 7428 5400
Fax: 020 7482 4851
Helpline: 0800 018 5026
www.oneparentfamilies.org.uk

One Parent Families Scotland
13 Gayfield Square,
Edinburgh EH1 3NX
Tel: 0131 556 3899
Fax: 0131 557 7899
Helpline: 0800 018 5026

Parentline Plus
Tel: 0808 800 2222
www.parentlineplus.org.uk

Parentline Scotland
Children 1st
83 Whitehouse Loan
Edinburgh
Tel: 0131 446 2300
Fax: 0131 446 2339
www.children1st.org.uk/parentline

Relate
Herbert Gray College,
Little Church Street, Rugby,
Warwickshire CV21 3AP
Tel: 0845 456 1310 or
01788 573241
Fax: 01788 535007
Helpline: 0845 130 4010
www.relate.org.uk

Salvation Army
101 Newington Causeway,
London SE1 6BN
Tel: 0845 634 0101
Fax: 020 7367 4728
www.salvationarmy.org.uk

Samaritans
The Upper Mill,
Kingston Road,
Ewell, Surrey, KT17 2AF
Tel: 020 8394 8300
Fax: 020 8394 8301
Helpline: 08457 909090
www.samaritans.org.uk

SANE
1st Floor, Cityside House,
40 Adler Street,
London E1 1EE
Tel: 020 7375 1002
Fax: 020 7375 2162
Helpline: 0845 767 8000
www.sane.org.uk

The Compassionate Friends (TCF)
53 North Street,
Bristol BS3 1EN
Tel: 0117 966 5202
Fax: 0117 914 4368
Helpline: 0117 953 9639
www.tcf.org.uk

Wing of Madness (for teenagers with depression)
www.wingofmadness.com/articles/teens.htm

YoungMinds
102-108 Clerkenwell Road,
London EC1M 5SA
Tel: 020 7336 8445
Fax: 020 7336 8446
Information Service:
0800 018 2138
www.youngminds.org.uk

Australian Bush Flower Essences

Most of the Australian Bush Flower Essences mentioned in this book are available in the UK from Revital—a health food store with three shops in London: in Willesden Green town centre, in Victoria opposite the British Airways Gatwick Check-in Terminal and in the London suburb of Ruislip.

Revital also offer shopping by post and online.

Products by post

Orders are taken by phone or fax on a free hotline number (0800-252-875) and merchandise is despatched within 12 hours—a free mail order catalogue is available.

Products by Internet

You can visit Revital's online store at the following website:

http://www.revital.com

or email them at:

enquire@revital.com

RECOMMENDED READING

Beal, G. W., and Hochman, G., *Adult Children of Divorce*, Delocarte Press, New York, 1991.

Eason, Cassandra, *Psychic Power of Children,* Foulsham, Berkshire, England, 1994.

Garth, Maureen, Starbright, *Children's Meditations,* Collins Dove, North Blackburn, Victoria, 1991.

BIBLIOGRAPHY

A-Z Alternative Therapy, Blitz Editions, Leicester, England, 1994.

Bennett, Dr. David, *Growing Pains*, Doubleday, Australia, 1987.

Clarke, Dr. J., *Advanced Professional Counselling*, Garrett Pty Ltd, Queensland, 1995.

Clarke, Dr. J., *Relationship Counselling*, Garrett Pty Ltd, Queensland, 1995.

Court, Dr. John, *You and Your Teenager*, Angus and Robertson, 1995.

Forward, Dr. Susan, *Toxic Parents*, Bantam, New York, 1990.

Holmes, Ernest, *The Science of Mind*, G. P. Putman & Sons, New York, 1988.

Irvine, John, with Warwick Irvine and Ian Wallace, *Coping with School*, Simon and Schuster, East Roseville, New South Wales, 1992.

Melody, Pia, *Facing Love Addiction*, Harper, San Francisco, 1992.

White, Ian, *Australian Bush Flower Essences*, Bantam Books, Sydney, 1991.

Pearson, Mark and Nolan, Patricia, *Emotional First Aid for Children*, Butterfly Books, Springwood, New South Wales, 1993.

Pearson, Mark and Nolan, Patricia, *Emotional Release for Children*, ACER, Melbourne, Victoria, 1995.

Pietroni, Prof. Patrick, *The Family Guide to Alternative Health*, The Book Company International Pty Ltd, Brookvale, New South Wales, 1995.

Pollard, Dr John III, *Self Parenting*, Generic Human Studies Publishing, California, 1987.

White, Judith, *Aromatherapy Blends for Life*, Blends for Life, Collingwood, Victoria, 1999.

INDEX TO MEDITATIONS AND AFFIRMATIONS

Meditations for children and teenagers listed by title

Meditations for adults and carers listed by title

Affirmations for children and teenagers listed by title

Affirmations for adults and carers listed by title

Meditations for children and teenagers listed by subject

Meditations for adults and carers listed by subject

Affirmations for children and teenagers listed by subject

Affirmations for adults and carers listed by subject